WITHDRAWN

JUN 2 7 2024

DAVID O. McKAY LIBRARY
BYU-IDAHO

THE KENT OF DICKENS

GAD'S HILL PLACE
DICKENS'S
KENTISH
HOME

Ω#214353

The
Kent of Dickens

BY

WALTER DEXTER

AUTHOR OF "THE LONDON OF DICKENS"

WITH FRONTISPIECE

PR 4584 .D4 1972
Dexter, Walter, 1877-1944.
The Kent of Dickens

PR 4584 .D4 1972
Dexter, Walter, 1877-1944.
The Kent of Dickens

HASKELL HOUSE PUBLISHERS Ltd.

Publishers of Scarce Scholarly Books

NEW YORK, N. Y. 10012

1972

RICKS COLLEGE
DAVID O. McKAY LR
REXBURG, IDAHO 83440

HASKELL HOUSE PUBLISHERS Ltd.

Publishers of Scarce Scholarly Books

280 LAFAYETTE STREET

NEW YORK. N. Y. 10012

Library of Congress Cataloging in Publication Data

Dexter, Walter, 1877-1944.
  The Kent of Dickens.

  1. Dickens, Charles, 1812-1870--Homes and haunts.
2. Literary landmarks--Kent. I. Title.
PR4584.D4 1972   823'.8 [B]   72-2105
ISBN 0-8383-1482-1

Printed in the United States of America

DICKENS'S ASSOCIATION WITH KENT

THE association of Dickens with Kent lasted throughout the whole of his life.

In 1816 when only four years of age, he came to live at Chatham at No. 2, Ordnance Terrace.

From 1821 to 1823, he lived at 18, St. Mary's Place, The Brook, Chatham, and at Chatham was his first school.

In his first success, *The Pickwick Papers*, Rochester is first among the towns visited by the Pickwickians. Maidstone (Muggleton), Gravesend, and Cobham are also introduced ; and in his last book *Edwin Drood*, Rochester, as Cloisterham, is the principal scene of the story.

In 1855, when at the height of his fame, he purchased Gad's Hill Place, near Rochester, the house he had longed for as a boy, and there he died in 1870.

At Broadstairs he spent the summers of 1837 to 1843, 1845, 1847 to 1851, and again visited it for a short time in 1859 ; and Folkestone was likewise visited for a seaside holiday in 1855. Canterbury was the home of Agnes Wickfield ; and Dover is indelibly associated with David Copperfield and his aunt.

" Kent, Sir—Everybody knows Kent—apples, cherries, hops and women."

Alfred Jingle (*Pickwick Papers*)

" Shall we go away that morning and stay in Kent ? "
Walter Gay (*Dombey and Son*)

" I have many happy recollections connected with Kent and am scarcely less interested in it than if I had been a Kentish man bred and born, and had resided in the county all my life."
Letter from Dickens, 1840

CONTENTS

THE CYCLIST'S OR MOTORIST'S ROUTE
THROUGH THE KENT OF DICKENS

	MILES		MILES
LONDON - - -		HYTHE - - - -	2¾
BLACKHEATH - - -	5	ASHFORD - - -	12
SHOOTER'S HILL - -	3	STAPLEHURST - - -	20
DARTFORD - - -	7	PADDOCK WOOD - -	12
NORTHFLEET - - -	5½	TUNBRIDGE WELLS -	6
GRAVESEND - - -	1½	TONBRIDGE - - -	5¾
CHALK - - - -	1¼	MAIDSTONE - - -	14¼
GAD'S HILL - - -	3	MALLING - - -	5
STROOD - - - -	2¼	AYLESFORD - - -	2
ROCHESTER - - -	½	SANDLING - - -	1½
CHATHAM - - -	1	BLUE BELL HILL - -	2½
SITTINGBOURNE - -	10	ROCHESTER - - -	4
CANTERBURY - - -	15¼	COBHAM - - - -	4
MARGATE - - -	16¼	SHORNE - - - -	2
BROADSTAIRS - - -	3½	GAD'S HILL - - -	1½
RAMSGATE - - -	2	HIGHAM - - -	1
PEGWELL - - -	7	COOLING - - -	5
DEAL - - - -	5½	CHALK - - - -	6
DOVER - - - -	8½	GRAVESEND - - -	1½
FOLKESTONE - - -	7	LONDON - - -	22
SANDGATE - - -	1¾	TOTAL - - -	237½

The Author desires to thank Mr. B. W. Matz, to whose Kentish articles in *The Dickensian*, of which he has been the Editor since its foundation in 1905, he is especially indebted ; also Messrs. Macmillan & Co., Ltd., for their kind permission to quote from the *Letters of Charles Dickens*

The Kent of Dickens

CHAPTER I

THE DOVER ROAD

" There's milestones on the Dover Road."
(Mr. F's. Aunt, *Little Dorrit*, Bk. I, Ch. XXIII)

I

THE road that leads from London to Dover is the backbone of Kent, the great highway famous alike in history and literature ; and Rochester, the centre pivot of the Kentish Dickens land, lies not quite half way between. The present chapter concerns the Dover Road as a whole, as Dickens saw it on his tramps between town and Gad's Hill ; as little David Copperfield saw it on his longer journey to his aunt's at Dover. Gravesend, Rochester, Chatham and Canterbury *en route*, are all dealt with separately.

The first few miles of the Dover Road—until Shooter's Hill is passed—is fully covered in the writer's *The London of Dickens*[1] to which readers must be referred for a full account of the interesting associations of Dickens with the Borough, Old Kent Road, Blackheath, and Greenwich.

[1] London : Cecil Palmer, Chandos Street, W.C

9

The Dover Road is measured from the south side of London Bridge and has its Dickens interest displayed throughout the whole length of its seventy odd miles, as the following table shows :

		Miles
Blackheath	- - -	5
Greenwich	- - -	6
Shooter's Hill	- -	8½
Dartford	- - - -	15
Northfleet	- - -	20¼
Gravesend	- - -	22
Chalk	- - -	23½
Gad's Hill	- - -	26¼
Strood	- - - -	28¼
Rochester	- - -	29
Chatham	- - -	30
Sittingbourne	- - -	40
Canterbury	- - -	55¼
Dover	- - -	70¾

Dickens's own experiences of the Dover Road are best shown by the following extracts from " Travelling Abroad " in *The Uncommercial Traveller* :

I got into the travelling chariot—it was of German make, roomy, heavy, and unvarnished —I got into the travelling chariot, pulled up the steps after me, shut myself in with a smart bang of the door, and gave the word, " Go on ! " Immediately, all that W. and S.W. division of London began to slide away at a pace so lively, that I was over the river, and past the Old Kent Road, and out on Blackheath, and even ascending Shooter's Hill, before I had had time to look about me in the carriage, like a collected traveller.

Over the road where the old Romans used to march, over the road where the old Canterbury pilgrims used to go, over the road where the travelling trains of the old imperious priests and princes used to jingle on horseback between the Continent and this Island through the mud and water, over the road where Shakespeare hummed to himself, " Blow, blow, thou winter wind," as he sat in the saddle at the gate of the inn yard noticing the carriers ; all among the cherry orchards, apple orchards, corn-fields and hop-gardens ; so went I, by Canterbury to Dover. There, the sea was tumbling in, with deep sounds, after dark, and the revolving French light on Cape Grinez was seen regularly bursting out and becoming obscured, as if the head of a gigantic light-keeper in an anxious state of mind were interposed every half minute, to look how it was burning.

His earlier recollections of a journey to London by coach also appear in the same book in the paper entitled " Dullborough Town," in which he recalls leaving Chatham for London at the age of eleven :

As I left Dullborough in the days when there were no railroads in the land, I left it in a stage coach . . . melodiously called Timpson's Blue-eyed Maid. . . . Timpson's was a moderate-sized coach office (in fact, a little coach office) with an oval transparency in the window, which looked beautiful by night, representing one of Timpson's coaches in the act of passing a mile-stone on the London road with great velocity.

It will be recalled that in *Little Dorrit*,

Mr. Arthur Clennam newly arrived from Marseilles by way of Dover, and by the Dover Coach, the Blue-eyed Maid.

In the concluding part of *The Seven Poor Travellers* we get another personal touch, and a true one, as

we know that Dickens often tramped the Dover
Road between Rochester and London.

As for me, I was going to walk by Cobham
Woods, as far upon my way to London as I
fancied. . . . Christmas begirt me, far and
near, until I had come to Blackheath, and had
walked down the long vista of gnarled old trees
in Greenwich Park and was being steam rattled
through the mists now closing in once more,
towards the lights of London.

II

The progress along the Dover Road, of the Dorrit
Family on one of the occasions when they left
London for the Continent after coming into their
riches, is thus recorded :

Next morning's sun saw Mr. Dorrit's equipage
upon the Dover Road, where every red-jacketed
postilion was the sign of a cruel house, estab-
lished for the unmerciful plundering of travellers.
The whole business of the human race between
London and Dover being spoliation, Mr. Dorrit
was waylaid at Dartford, pillaged at Gravesend,
rifled at Rochester, fleeced at Sittingbourne,
and sacked at Canterbury.

It was along the Dover Road—between Rochester
and London—that Pip journeyed many times ;
notably when first in receipt of his Great Expectations he came up to London :

The journey from our town to the metropolis,
was a journey of about five hours. It was a
little past midday when the four horse stage
coach by which I was a passenger, got into the
ravel of traffic frayed out about the Cross Keys,
Wood Street, Cheapside, London ;

and again when he made the first journey home in company with the convicts, and heard the reference to the " Two One Pound notes." Towards the close of the book he again tells us :

I went down again by the coach next day. But I alighted at the Half-way House, and breakfasted there, and walked the rest of the distance.

There are several half-way houses on the Dover Road : houses of call half way from everywhere to anywhere, as behoves a road so ancient in tired travellers, and Dickens had one of them in view when introducing us to the " sagacious Bunsby " in *Dombey and Son*, for we are told that his " eye continued to be addressed to somewhere about the half-way house between London and Gravesend."

In an early chapter of *A Tale of Two Cities* we are introduced to the Dover Road in a brilliant piece of descriptive writing describing the mail coach and the fear of its conductors and passengers of the highwaymen that beset the road at the time of which the story deals.

It was the Dover Road that lay, on a Friday night late in November, before the first of the persons with whom this history has business. The Dover Road lay, as to him, beyond the Dover Mail, as it lumbered up Shooter's Hill.

In the trial of Charles Darnay for high treason in the same book we find a further reference to the Dover Road :

Charles Darnay had . . . pleaded Not Guilty to an indictment denouncing him . . . for that he was a false traitor. . . . The prisoner went down . . . in the Dover Mail . . . got out of the mail in the night, as a blind, at a place where he did not remain, but from which he travelled

back some dozen miles or more, to a garrison
and dockyard, and there collected information.
It is not difficult to see from this that the garrison
referred to was Chatham.

In the various ruses employed by Pip and Herbert
in *Great Expectations* to hide the tracks of his so-
called Uncle Provis, *alias* the returned convict
Magwitch, we read that on one occasion it was
given out that he had gone to Dover, for which
purpose " he was taken down the Dover Road and
cornered out of it."

In *Pickwick*, referring to the salutation between
the elder Mr. Weller and his friends, which we are
told consisted of a " jerking round of the right
wrist and a rising of the little finger into the air at
the same time," a salutation " strictly confined to
the freemasonry of the craft," the following is
narrated :

We once knew two famous coachmen who were
twins, and between whom an unaffected and
devoted attachment existed. They passed each
other on the Dover Road, every day, for twenty-
four years, never exchanging any other greeting
than this ; and yet, when one died, the other
pined away, and soon afterwards followed him.

The best account of the Dover Road is of course
that given in Chapter XIII of *David Copperfield*,
detailing the walk of little David to his aunt's at
Dover.   After being robbed of his box and his half
guinea, at the Obelisk, Blackfriars Road, we read :

I ran after him as fast as I could. . . . I
narrowly escaped being run over, twenty times
at least, in half a mile. . . . At length, confused by fright and heat, and doubting whether
half London might not by this time be turning
out for my apprehension, I left the young man

to go where he would with my box and money ;
and, panting and crying, but never stopping,
faced about for Greenwich, which I had understood was on the Dover Road. . . .

For anything I know, I may have had some
wild idea of running all the way to Dover, when
I gave up the pursuit of the young man with the
donkey-cart, and started for Greenwich.

That night he slept at Blackheath beneath a
haystack within sight of his old school, Salem
House, and the next day, Sunday, he writes :

I crept into the long dusty track which I had
first known to be the Dover Road when I was
one of them [i.e. Mr. Creakle's boys] and when
I little expected that any eyes would ever see
me the wayfarer I was now, upon it. . . . I
got that Sunday through three-and-twenty miles
on the straight road, though not very easily,
for I was new to that kind of toil.

He crossed over Rochester Bridge that evening
and slept in Chatham, " near a cannon . . . upon
a sort of grass-grown battery overhanging a lane,
where a sentry was walking to and fro." The
following day he sold his jacket there, after a deal
of trouble, to the dreadful old man with his lungs
and his liver and his goroo goroo, who eventually
bid him " go for fourpence " more.

I was so faint and weary that I closed with
this offer . . . and limped seven miles upon
my road. My bed at night was under another
haystack. . . . When I took the road again
next morning, I found that it lay through a
succession of hop grounds and orchards. . . .
I thought it extremely beautiful and made up
my mind to sleep among the hops that night,
imagining some cheerful companionship in the

long perspective of poles, with the graceful leaves twining round them.

This must have brought him to about Newington, thirty-seven miles from London. It was on the Tuesday morning that he fell in with the tramping tinker, probably near Sittingbourne, where Mr. Dorrit is described as being " fleeced " during his grand progress to Dover. That night he slept among the hops again, and in the heat of the following day passed through the sunny streets of Canterbury (see page 160). Wednesday night he must have spent somewhere between Canterbury and Dover, because he tells us that he wore away all the morning at Dover (see page 211) enquiring for the place of residence of his aunt, and he calls it the sixth day of his flight.

On the occasion when David returned by coach along the same road under happier auspices, and had the conversation with the coachman about the Suffolk Punches, which occasioned what he always considered to be his first fall in life, he reviewed the scene in the following :

It was curious and interesting, nevertheless, to be sitting up there, behind four horses : well educated, well dressed, and with plenty of money in my pocket ; and to look out for the places where I had slept on my weary journey. I had abundant occupation for my thoughts, in every conspicuous landmark on the road. When I looked down at the tramps whom we passed, and saw that well-remembered style of face turned up, I felt as if the tinker's blackened hand were in the bosom of my shirt again. When we clattered through the narrow street of Chatham, and I caught a glimpse, in passing, of the lane where the old monster lived, who had bought my jacket, I stretched my neck eagerly to look for the place where I had sat, in the sun and in the shade, waiting for my money. When we came, at last, within a stage of London, and passed the veritable Salem House where Mr. Creakle had laid about him with a heavy hand, I would have given all I had, for lawful permission to get down and thrash him, and let all the boys out like so many caged sparrows.

III

The first name associating Dickens with the Borough is that of the " White Hart," where Sam Weller was discovered by Mr. Pickwick, who had come here from Manor Farm near Rochester (see page 72) on the track of Alfred Jingle who had eloped with Rachael Wardle. We do not claim that it was on the Dover Road that the chase, described in Chapter IX, took place ; most probably the road was the Folkestone Road via Farningham and Sidcup ; but the latter portion of the road—from New Cross to the Borough—would be common to both roads.

The Borough ends at Saint George's Church, close by which stood the Marshalsea Prison, in which the elder Dickens was imprisoned for debt, and where, years afterwards, Little Dorrit was born. Here we turn to the left and soon reach the Old Kent Road, joining the road from the Elephant and Castle, Westminster Bridge, and Charing Cross, along which came the " Commodore " coach bearing the Pickwickians on their first recorded journey—to Rochester. The Dover Road continues to New Cross through Deptford, over Blackheath, up Shooter's Hill and then through Bexley, Crayford,

2

and Dartford. Unfortunately there is no record in *Pickwick* of any place on the Dover Road until Rochester is reached, except the following :

> In this strain, with an occasional glass of ale by way of parenthesis, when the coach changed horses, did the stranger proceed until they reached Rochester Bridge.

Dartford was doubtless the stopping place in question, and the Bull Inn there is outwardly almost an exact replica of its famous brother at Rochester.

An account of a visit to Dartford paid by Dickens and Mark Lemon in 1854 is given in a characteristic letter from Dickens to W. H. Wills, dated 12th April, 1854 :

> Mark and I walked to Dartford from Greenwich, last Monday, and found Mrs. . . . acting " The Stranger " (with a strolling company from the Standard Theatre) in Mr. Munn's schoolroom. The stage was a little wider than your table here, and its surface was composed of loose boards laid on the school forms. Dogs sniffed about it during the performances, and the carpenter's highlows were ostentatiously taken off and displayed in the proscenium.
>
> We stayed until a quarter to ten, when we were obliged to fly to the railroad, but we sent the landlord of the hotel down with the following articles :
>
> 1. bottle superior old port,
> 1. do.   do. golden sherry,
> 1. do.   do. best French brandy,
> 1. do.   do. 1st quality Old Tom gin,
> 1. do.   do. prime Jamaica rum,
> 1. do.   do. small still Isla whiskey,
> 1. kettle boiling water, two pounds finest white lump sugar,

Our cards,
1. lemon
     and
Our compliments.

The effect we had previously made upon the theatrical company by being beheld in the first two chairs—there was nearly a pound in the house—was altogether electrical.

Just before reaching Gravesend we come to Northfleet, referred to by Mr. Inspector in his investigations of the Harmon mystery when he is instructing Mortimer Lightwood and Eugene Wrayburn in the part they have to play :

You can't do better than be interested in some lime works anywhere down about North-fleet, and doubtful whether some of your lime don't get into bad company, as it comes up in Barges.

In Northfleet were Rosherville Gardens, a very popular resort in the Victorian era ; of a contemplated visit to these gardens Dickens refers in a letter to Miss Power dated, 2nd July, 1847 :

Ah Rosherville ! That fated Rosherville, when shall we see it ! Perhaps in one of those intervals when I am up to town from here, and suddenly appear at Gore House, somebody will propose an excursion there, next day. If anybody does, somebody else will be ready to go. So this deponent maketh oath and saith.

In *The Uncommercial Traveller* paper on "Tramps" there is an interesting account of the class of tramp to be met with on the Dover Road, whom Dickens doubtless knew well :

There is another kind of tramp, whom you encounter this bright summer day—say, on a road with the sea-breeze making its dust lively,

and sails of ships in the blue distance beyond
the slope of Down. As you walk enjoyingly
on, you descry in the perspective at the bottom
of a steep hill up which your way lies, a figure
that appears to be sitting airily on a gate,
whistling in a cheerful and disengaged manner.
As you approach nearer to it, you observe the
figure to slide down from the gate, to desist
from whistling, to uncock its hat, to become
tender of foot, to depress its head and elevate
its shoulders, and to present all the characteris-
tics of profound despondency. Arriving at the
bottom of the hill and coming close to the figure,
you observe it to be the figure of a shabby
young man. He is moving painfully forward,
in the direction in which you are going, and his
mind is so preoccupied with his misfortunes that
he is not aware of your approach until you are
close upon him at the hill-foot. He says in a
flowing confidential voice, and without punctua-
tion, " I ask your pardon sir but if you would
excuse the liberty of being so addressed upon the
public Iway by one who is almost reduced to
rags though it as not always been so and by no
fault of his own but through ill elth in his family
and many unmerited sufferings it would be a
great obligation sir to know the time." You
give the well-spoken young man the time. The
well-spoken young man, keeping well up with
you, resumes : " I am aware sir that it is a
liberty to intrude a further question on a
gentleman walking for his entertainment but
might I make so bold as ask the favour
of the way to Dover sir and about the
distance ? " You inform   the   well-spoken
young man that the way to Dover is straight

on, and the distance some eighteen miles. The well-spoken young man becomes greatly agitated. " In the condition to which I am reduced," says he, " I could not ope to reach Dover before dark even if my shoes were in a state to take me there or my feet were in a state to old out over the flinty road and were not on the bare ground of which any gentleman has the means to satisfy himself by looking . . . Sir I implore you in the name of charity to purchase a tortoiseshell comb which is a genuine article at any price that your humanity may put upon it and may the blessings of a ouseless family awaiting with beating arts the return of a husband and a father from Dover upon the cold stone seats of London bridge ever attend you Sir may I take the liberty of speaking to you I implore you to buy this comb ! " By this time, being a reasonably good walker, you will have been too much for the well-spoken young man, who will stop short and express his disgust and his want of breath, in a long expectoration, as you leave him behind.

The whereabouts of the Tilted Wagon, the "roadside tavern" . . . eight miles away from Cloisterham, whither Neville Landless walked on the morning after the disappearance of Edwin Drood, thus arousing grave suspicions, has not yet been made known. It was described as

a cool establishment on the top of a hill, where the ground before the door was puddled with damp hoofs and trodden straw ; where a scolding landlady slapped a moist baby (with one red sock on and one wanting), in the bar ; where the cheese was cast aground upon a shelf, in company with a mouldy tablecloth and a

greenhandled knife, in a sort of cast-iron
canoe ; where the palefaced bread shed tears
of crumb over its shipwreck in another canoe ;
where the family linen, half washed and half
dried, led a public life of lying about ; where
anything to drink was drunk out of mugs, and
everything else was suggestive of a rhyme to mugs.

It has been suggested that Dickens had in view
the Coach and Horses Inn at the top of Strood Hill
when writing the above description, but he penned
a picture typical of any roadside public-house, and
it is not always wise to think that Dickens had one
particular place in view when writing.

IV

We will conclude our account of Dickens's
association with the Dover Road generally (before
entering upon details of the better-known portions
of it) with an extract from *Charles Dickens as I
knew Him* by his manager for the Reading tours,
George Dolby, who wrote from intimate knowledge :

" As for Dickens himself, the weather very seldom
kept him from the pedestrian exercises, of which
he was so fond ; and many a misty walk we took
to the marshes at Cooling, that we might get a
realistic notion of the dreariness and loneliness of
the scenes in *Great Expectations*, made famous
by ' Pip ' and the convict. On such occasions as
these we not unfrequently returned wetted to the
skin by a drenching rain.

" One of the most delightful days of this visit was
occupied by a drive from Gad's Hill to Canterbury,
a distance of twenty-nine miles, over the old Dover
Road, through Rochester, Chatham, Sittingbourne,
and Faversham.

" We were to make an early start, so as to give plenty of time for luncheon, in a beautiful spot already chosen, and allow for a ramble afterwards.

" Two post carriages were turned out with postilions, in the red jackets of the old Royal Dover Road, buck-skin breeches, and top-boots into the bargain.

" The preparations for this new pilgrimage to Canterbury were of the most lavish description, and I can see now the hampers and wine baskets blocking the steps of the house before they were packed in the carriages.

" Every one was in the best of spirits, the weather was all that could be desired, and the ladies did honour to it by the brightness of their costumes. We were all glad, too, that the restoration of the Chief's health enabled him to enjoy as much pleasure himself as he was giving to his friends.

" We started sharp to time, and travelled merrily over the road, with hop-gardens on either side, until we reached Rochester, our horses making such a clatter in this slumbrous old city that all the shop-keepers in the main street turned out to see us pass.

" Mr. Dickens rode in the foremost carriage, and having occasion to pull up at the shop of one of the tradesmen in the main street of Rochester, a small crowd collected round the carriages. It seemed to be pretty generally known amongst them that Dickens was of the party, and we got a good deal of fun out of the mistake made by a man in the crowd, who pointed up at Mr. James T. Fields, and called out, ' That's Dickens ! ' Poor Fields was in great confusion, especially when Mr. Dickens, to com-plete the deception, handed up a small parcel to him, with the request, ' Here you are, Dickens, take charge of this for me.'

" Away we went again through Rochester, and, skirting Chatham, were soon again in the open country on the road to Sittingbourne, where a relay of horses was awaiting us.

" A short rest in the brick-making town was quite sufficient for us, and we sped on to that haven of rest where it had been arranged that we should lunch. A more suitable spot could not have been found. It lay in the deep shades of a wood, with a rippling stream running through.

" The breakfast hour had been an early one, and the long drive had given an excellent edge to our appetites. We turned to with a ready will to unload the carriages, and carry the baskets into the wood. Everybody did something, and the cloth was speedily laid. An hour was the time allowed for luncheon, and out of this we had to let the postilions get their meal when we had finished. Dickens would not let us start again until every vestige of our visit to the wood in the shape of lobster shells and other debris, had been removed.

.   .   .   .   .   .

" There was never a more delightful ride on a summer's evening than the one we took then. The day was fast closing in, and as there was no reason for loitering on the road, we sped along at a rattling pace.

" The journey from Gad's Hill to Canterbury had taken nearly five hours, including the time allowed for luncheon and loitering. The journey home was made in less than three, and we forgot our fatigue in the enjoyment of supper. It seems to me, as I look back over the years that have intervened, that I enjoyed a great privilege, no less than a rare pleasure, in being in the company of my dear old

Chief when he took this his last visit to Canterbury, in the streets of which he had so often wandered in his earlier days.

" The next day, the red-jacketed postilions were ordered out again, and we commenced with a visit to Chatham, which in an æsthetic point of view is not an interesting place. The streets are very narrow and most consumedly dirty. But if the town itself be disagreeable, the society is very much the reverse. Mr. Dickens had many friend among the naval and military officers and their families, whom duty compels to exist in that objectionable place, and of these, none whom he valued more than the general commanding the district at the time—General Freeman Murray.

" In compliment to Mr. Dickens and his American friends, the general had organized an early reception at his house, in the grounds of which he had provided us with a military band.

" The general conducted us through some of the barracks, and we visited several of the officers in their quarters, returning to Gad's Hill for luncheon. General Murray, who made one of the party, afterwards had his drag out, and gave us a most enjoyable drive. He brought us home through Cobham Park, where, disdaining the roadways, he made short cuts across the level turf, dodging in and out under the magnificent trees, which made it rather lively for the general's outside passengers. But the general is an excellent whip, and nobody was killed."

CHAPTER II

GRAVESEND AND CHALK

" We come you see . . . in one of our Yarmouth lugs to Gravesen'."

(Mr. Peggotty in *David Copperfield*)

I

GRAVESEND finds but little mention in Dickens's novels, in spite of the fact that Gad's Hill lies midway between it and Rochester, and was known to Dickens very well indeed ; even such references as are made are but casual.

Many like to imagine that Gravesend was the Muggleton of *The Pickwick Papers*, but, although Muggleton is doubtless a compound of more than one town, it is not likely that the place through which the Pickwickians had passed *en route* for Rochester would be treated later on as a new town hitherto unknown to Mr. Pickwick and his friends.

Dickens was not unfamiliar with Gravesend. At Chalk, a mile out of the town on the road to Rochester, he spent his honeymoon (see page 30). He stayed a day and a night there with Forster in 1841, and in a letter to Wilkie Collins, dated Tavistock House, 17th December, 1854, there is an allusion to a visit to Gravesend, and to riding home at night in a hansom. He spent some time here during the repairs and decorations of Gad's Hill in 1857, and wrote from Gravesend saying, " As I am away from London for a few days

26

your letter was forwarded to me." He stayed at Waite's Hotel, now the Commercial Hotel, on the Gordon Promenade. And a few days later (15th April) we find him still at Gravesend penning a letter to Lord Carlisle, commencing, " I am writing by the river side for a few days " ; but his real object was to superintend the alterations at Gad's Hill Place.

Gravesend used to be a holiday resort in Dickens's day. In *Bleak House* we are told how, in the long vacation,

> the hottest long vacation known for many years, all the young clerks are madly in love, and . . . pine for bliss with the beloved object, at Margate, Ramsgate or Gravesend ;

and in the *Sketches by Boz* (" Tuggses at Ramsgate"), Mr. Joseph Tuggs suggested Gravesend as the place for the family holiday, but " the idea was unanimously scouted. Gravesend was *low*."

When Joe Willet enlisted,

> the party embarked in a passage boat bound for Gravesend, whence they were to proceed on foot to Chatham ;

and in the same book, Gabriel Varden suggests to his wife that Sim Tappertit should be got away by " the Gravesend tide boat " from the Tower Stairs, and so to Canterbury, where Mrs. Varden's cousin would provide him with work until the storm of the rioting had blown over—a suggestion Sim indignantly repels.

Mr. Peggotty and Ham, when visiting David Copperfield at Salem House, Blackheath, came from Yarmouth via Gravesend by water.

> We come you see, the wind and tide making in our favour, in one of our Yarmouth lugs to Gravesen'. My sister she wrote to me the name of this here place, and wrote to me as if I ever

chanced to come to Gravesen' I was to come
over and enquire for Mas'r Davy.

In later years, when Mr. Peggotty emigrated with
Mr. Micawber, the vessel sailed from Gravesend.

In the afternoon of the next day, my old
nurse and I went down to Gravesend. We
found the ship in the river surrounded by a
crowd of boats. . . . Mr. Peggotty was waiting
for us on deck.

And when the party sailed and David left for the
shore, he tells us :

The night had fallen on the Kentish hills
when we were rowed ashore—and fallen darkly
upon me.

After his tour on the Continent, David writes
of his return, landing at Gravesend :

Three years had elapsed since the sailing of
the emigrant ship ; when at that same hour of
sunset, and in the same place, I stood on the deck
of the packet vessel that brought me home,
looking on the rosy water where I had seen the
image of that boat reflected.

Jack Malden in the same book left for India by a
steamer from Gravesend ; and later, Julia Mills
sailed from the same port :

Dora and I had gone aboard a great East
Indiaman at Gravesend to see her ; and we had
had preserved ginger, and guava, and other
delicacies of that sort for lunch ; and we had
left Miss Mills weeping on a camp-stool on the
quarter-deck, with a large new diary under her
arm, in which the original reflections awakened
by the contemplation of Ocean were to be
recorded under lock and key.

Gravesend too was the port of embarkation of
Walter Gay and his wife Florence Dombey.

Shall we go away that morning, and stay in Kent until we go on board at Gravesend within a week ? he asks her.

That " Monument of great antiquity " (" Bill Stumps his mark ") discovered by Mr. Pickwick at Cobham (page 58) was disposed of via Gravesend :

After a hearty breakfast, the four gentlemen sallied forth to walk to Gravesend, followed by a man bearing the stone in its deal box. They reached that town about one o'clock (their luggage they had directed to be forwarded to the City, from Rochester), and being fortunate enough to secure places on the outside of a coach, arrived in London in sound health and spirits on that same afternoon.

II

The scene of the exploit of Pip and Herbert to get the convict Magwitch out of the country was on the river below Gravesend.

I had always proposed to myself to get him well down the river in the boat ; certainly well beyond Gravesend, which was a critical place for search or enquiry if suspicions were afloat.

Our plan was this. The tide beginning to run down at nine and being with us until three, we intended still to creep on after it had turned, and row against it until dark. We should then be well in those long reaches below Gravesend, between Kent and Essex, where the river is broad, and solitary, where the waterside inhabitants are very few, and where lone public-houses are scattered here and there, of which we could well choose one for a resting place. There, we meant to lie by, all night.

The little public-house where they stayed the
night, and from which they set off to board the
Rotterdam steamer, is said to be the " Ship and
Lobster." My friend Colonel Gadd of Gravesend
has traced out the course, and is convinced that
the original of the Ship was The Lobster Smack at
Canvey Island, which certainly fits in better with what
takes place than any public-house near Gravesend.

Dickens describes it as

a dirty place enough and I dare say not unknown
to smuggling adventurers. . . . The wind had
risen, and the sign of the house (the Ship) was
creaking and banging about.

It was to the same public-house that Magwitch
returned under arrest, on his way to his trial in
London.

III

The village of Chalk is at the eastern end of
Gravesend, about a mile from the town. It was
here that Dickens spent his honeymoon in 1836.
The house where the newly married couple stayed
is generally supposed to be the large one on the
south side of the road at the corner of Thong Lane.
Laman Blanchard has left it on record that he used
often to meet Dickens at this spot, and " here the
brisk walk of Charles Dickens was always slackened,
and he never failed to glance meditatively for a
few moments at the windows of a corner house on
the southern side of the road, advantageously
situated for commanding views of the river and the
far stretching landscapes beyond. It was in that
house he lived immediately after his marriage."

This house was unquestioned until about 1905,
when inquiries were set on foot and investigations
made with a view to marking the house with a

memorial tablet. It was then found that the Manor House—as it was called—had never been let to lodgers—being in the occupation of a doctor, and that the real house was a cottage on the opposite side of the road, nearer Gravesend.

Two tablets were affixed there by the Gravesend Branch of the Dickens Fellowship, and unveiled by the Mayor on 14th June, 1911.

(1) A gun-metal tablet on the north side bearing the inscription :

In this house Charles Dickens spent his honeymoon in 1836 ; here also some early chapters of " Pickwick " were written.

(2) A marble plate with bronze plaque of Dickens, executed and presented by Mr. Percy Fitzgerald, and placed over the doorway. The inscription reads :

Charles Dickens, Born 1812. Died 1870.
Spent his Honeymoon in this house (1836).
Here also were written some early chapters of Pickwick.

Dickens was very partial to putting his characters in the position he had once occupied, so we find that both Walter Gay in *Dombey and Son* and Tommy Traddles in *David Copperfield* spent their honeymoons in Kent.

Chalk Church is a landmark hereabouts ; over the porch is a curious carving which Forster tells us used to attract Dickens's attention when he walked this way from Gad's Hill :

" He would walk through the marshes to Gravesend, return by Chalk Church, and stop always to have greeting with a comical old monk who for some incomprehensible reason sits carved in stone cross-legged with a jovial pot, over the porch of that sacred edifice."

CHAPTER III

GAD'S HILL

" My little Kentish Freehold."
(Dickens, in a letter to Cerjat)

I

ON the high ground of the main Dover Road, almost midway between Gravesend and Rochester, standing a little way back on the right, is the house that is familiarly and affectionately known to the innumerable band of Dickens devotees the world over as Gad's Hill, its full and correct name being Gad's Hill Place. This was Dickens's home from 1857 until his death in 1870.

But years before it became his home—indeed from his very earliest years when a small boy at Chatham—he conceived a great attachment to the house. He used to like to be taken out to see it by his father, and it was a cherished ambition of his life to be in a position to buy the house and live there.

He has confirmed this in his paper " Travelling Abroad " in *The Uncommercial Traveller*, in which as he is journeying along the road to Dover there crosses it a vision of himself :

So smooth was the old high road, and so fresh were the horses, and so fast went I, that it was midway between Gravesend and Rochester, and the widening river was bearing the ships,

white-sailed or black-smoked, out to sea, when
I noticed by the wayside a very queer small boy.

" Holloa ! " said I, to the very queer small
boy, " where do you live ? "

" At Chatham," says he.

" What do you do there ? " says I.

" I go to school," says he.

I took him up in a moment, and we went on.
Presently, the very queer small boy says,
" This is Gadshill we are coming to, where
Falstaff went out to rob those travellers, and
ran away."

" You know something about Falstaff, eh ? "
said I.

" All about him," said the very queer small
boy. " I am old (I am nine), and I read all sorts
of books. But *do* let us stop at the top of the
hill, and look at the house there, if you please ! "

" You admire that house ? " said I.

" Bless you, sir," said the very queer small
boy, " when I was not more than half as old as
nine, it used to be a treat for me to be brought
to look at it. And now I am nine, I come by
myself to look at it. And ever since I can
recollect, my father, seeing me so fond of it,
has often said to me, *If you were to be very per-
severing, and were to work hard, you might some
day come to live in it.* Though that's impossible !"
said the very queer small boy, drawing a low
breath, and now staring at the house out of
window with all his might.

I was rather amazed to be told this by the
very queer small boy ; for that house happens
to be *my* house, and I have reason to believe
that what he said was true.

Before he had come to be able to purchase the

3

house, he had already introduced it into at least one of his books, as the following extract from *A Christmas Carol* will show :

" Good Heavens," said Scrooge. . . . " I was born in this place. I was a boy here." . . .

" You recollect that ? " enquired the Spirit. " Remember it," cried Scrooge. . . . " I could walk it blindfold. . . ."

They walked along the road, Scrooge recognising every gate and post and tree until a little market town appeared in the distance, with its bridge, its church and widening river. . . .

They left the high road by a well-remembered lane and soon approached a mansion of dull red brick, with a little weathercock-surmounted cupola on the roof, and a bell hanging in it. It was a large house, but one of broken fortunes.

II

His ambition was gratified in 1855 at the age of forty-three. Writing to W. H. Wills on the 9th February, 1855 (Wills was the assistant editor of *Household Words*), he said :

I want to alter the arrangements for to-morrow, and put you to some inconvenience.

When I was at Gravesend t'other day, I saw, at Gad's Hill—just opposite to the Hermitage, where Miss Lynn used to live—a little freehold to be sold. The spot and the very house are literally " a dream of my childhood," and I should like to look at it before I go to Paris. With that purpose I must go to Strood by the North Kent, at a quarter-past ten to-morrow morning, and I want you, strongly booted, to go with me ! (I know the particulars from the agent.)

Can you ? Let me know. If you can, can you manage so that we can take the proofs with us ? If you can't, will you bring them to Tavistock House at dinner time to-morrow, half-past five ? Forster will dine with us, but no one else.

A few days later he wrote to Forster from Paris :

I was better pleased with Gadshill Place last Saturday, on going down there, even than I had prepared myself to be. The country, against every disadvantage of season, is beautiful ; and the house is so old-fashioned, cheerful, and comfortable, that it is really pleasant to look at. The good old Rector now there, has lived in it six and twenty years, so I have not the heart to turn him out. He is to remain till Lady-Day next year, when I shall go in, please God ; make my alterations ; furnish the house ; and keep it for myself that summer ;

and we find another letter on the same subject on his return to England in the July, when he had passed through Kent, and was pleased to see what progress had been made in local railway construction :

A railroad opened from Rochester to Maidstone, which connects Gadshill at once with the whole sea coast, is certainly an addition to the place, and an enhancement of its value. Bye and bye we shall have the London, Chatham and Dover, too ; and that will bring it within an hour of Canterbury and an hour and a half of Dover. I am glad to hear of your having been in the neighbourhood. There is no healthier (marshes avoided), and none in my eyes more beautiful. One of these days I shall show you some places up the Medway with which you will be charmed.

In the meantime he had completed the purchase on the 14th March, on which occasion he wrote to Forster :

This day I have paid the purchase-money for Gadshill Place. After drawing the cheque (£1790) I turned round to give it to Wills, and said, " Now isn't it an extraordinary thing— look at the Day—Friday ! I have been nearly drawing it half-a-dozen times when the lawyers have not been ready, and here it comes round on a Friday as a matter of course."

The great pleasure he felt at the possession of the house so long coveted is shown in the letter which he wrote to his French friend Monsieur Cerjat, on the 17th January, 1856 :

Down at Gad's Hill, near Rochester, in Kent— Shakespeare's Gad's Hill, where Falstaff engaged in the robbery—is a quaint little country-house of Queen Anne's time. I happened to be walking past, a year and a half or so ago, with my sub-editor of *Household Words,* when I said to him, " You see that house ? It has always a curious interest for me, because when I was a small boy down in these parts I thought it the most beautiful house (I suppose because of its famous old cedar-trees) ever seen. And my poor father used to bring me to look at it, and used to say that if I ever grew up to be a clever man perhaps I might own that house, or such another house. In remembrance of which, I have always in passing looked to see if it was to be sold or let, and it has never been to me like any other house, and it has never changed at all." We came back to town, and my friend went out to dinner. Next morning he came to me in great excitement, and said : " It is written that you were to have that house at Gad's Hill. The lady I had allotted to me to take down to dinner yesterday began to speak of that neighbourhood. ' You know it ? ' I said ; ' I have been there to-day.' ' O yes,' said she, ' I know it very well. I was a child there, in the house they call Gad's Hill Place. My father was the rector, and lived there many years. He has just died, has left it to me, and I want to sell it.' So," says the sub-editor, " you must buy it. Now or never ! " I did, and hope to pass next summer there, though I may, perhaps, let it afterwards, furnished, from time to time.

During the year 1857 somewhat extensive altera- tions were carried out before the house was ready to be occupied, and to superintend the commence- ment of these he stayed for a week or more at Waite's Hotel in Gravesend (see page 27), from which place he wrote to Lord Carlisle on 15th April :

On the tip top of Gad's Hill, between this and Rochester, on the very spot where Falstaff ran away, I have a pretty little old-fashioned house, which I shall live in the hope of showing to you one day.

In the July he wrote to Forster that the altera- tions were still unfinished :

We are still boring for water here at the rate of two pounds per day for Wages. The men seem to like it very much.

In the following September there were three characteristic letters to Forster, on the district and the repairs. The first is dated the 5th :

Hop-picking is going on, and people sleep in

the garden, and breathe in at the keyhole of the house door. I have been amazed, before this year, by the number of miserable lean wretches, hardly able to crawl, who go hop-picking. I find it is a superstition that the dust of the newly-picked hop, falling freshly into the throat, is a cure for consumption. So the poor creatures drag themselves along the roads, and sleep under wet hedges, and get cured soon and finally.

Then on the 24th, Dickens still found himself in the throes of the well sinkers.

Here are six men perpetually going up and down the well (I know that somebody will be killed), in the course of fitting a pump : which is quite a railway terminus—it is so iron and so big. The process is much more like putting Oxford Street endwise, and laying gas along it, than anything else. By the time it is finished, the cost of this water will be something absolutely frightful. But of course it proportionately increases the value of the property, and that's my only comfort. . . . The horse has gone lame from a sprain, the big dog has run a ten-penny nail into one of his hind feet, the bolts have all flown out of the basket-carriage, and the gardener says all the fruit trees want replacing with new ones.

These troubles, inseparable from the desire to make the place as completely habitable as ever possible, had their recompense in the beautiful country Dickens was now able to enjoy to the full, for he wrote to Forster on 27th September :

I have discovered that the seven miles between Maidstone and Rochester is one of the most beautiful walks in England.

In July, 1858, we find him again writing to Monsieur Cerjat :

At this present moment I am on my little Kentish free-hold (not in top-boots, and not particularly prejudiced that I know of), looking on as pretty a view out of my study window as you will find in a long day's English ride. My little place is a grave red brick house (time of George the First, I suppose), which I have added to and stuck bits upon in all manner of ways, so that it is as pleasantly irregular, and as violently opposed to all architectural ideas, as the most hopeful man could possibly desire. It is on the summit of Gad's Hill. The robbery was committed before the door, on the man with the treasure, and Falstaff ran away from the identical spot of ground now covered by the room in which I write. A little rustic alehouse, called the Sir John Falstaff, is over the way— has been over the way, ever since, in honour of the event. Cobham Woods and Park are behind the house ; the distant Thames in front ; the Medway, with Rochester, and its old castle and cathedral on one side. The whole stupendous property is on the old Dover Road, so when you come, come by the North Kent Railway (not the South-Eastern) to Strood or Higham, and I'll drive over to fetch you.

To another French friend, Monsieur Regnier, he wrote (16th November, 1859) :

My Gad's Hill house (I think I omitted to tell you, in reply to your enquiry) is on the very scene of Falstaff's robbery. There is a little cabaret at the roadside, still called The Sir John Falstaff. And the country, in all its general features, is at this time, what it was in

Shakespeare's. I hope you will see the house before long. It is really a pretty place, and a good residence for an English writer, is it not ?

III

It was not until the autumn of 1860 that his furniture and books were sent from Tavistock House, London, and the occupation of the house begun in earnest. At this time we find him writing to Forster :

When you come down here next month, we have an idea that we shall show you rather a neat house. What terrific adventures have been in action ; how many overladen vans were knocked up at Gravesend, and had to be dragged out of Chalk-turnpike in the dead of the night by the whole equine power of this establishment ; shall be revealed at another time.

In the entrance hall to the house still hangs the original framed greeting with which his many friends were welcomed to his new abode :

THIS HOUSE, GADSHILL PLACE, stands on the summit of Shakespeare's Gadshill, ever memorable for its association with Sir John Falstaff in his noble fancy. *But, my lads, my lads, to-morrow morning, by four o'clock, early at Gadshill ! there are pilgrims going to Canterbury with rich offerings, and traders riding to London with fat purses : I have vizards for you all ; you have horses for yourselves.*

It was the pride of Dickens's life to show the house to his friends and entertain them there. Forster tells us in his *Life of Dickens* :

" When such friends as Longfellow and his daughters, or Charles Eliot Norton and his wife, came, or when Mr. Fields brought his wife and Professor Lowell's daughter, or when he received other Americans to whom he owed special courtesy, he would compress into infinitely few days an enormous amount of sight seeing and country enjoyment, castles, cathedrals, and fortified lines, lunches and picnics among cherry orchards and hop-gardens, excursions to Canterbury or Maidstone and their beautiful neighbourhoods, Druid-stone and Blue Bell Hill. ' All the neighbouring country that could be shown in so short a time,' he wrote of the Longfellow visit, ' they saw. I turned out a couple of postilions in the old red jackets of the old red royal Dover road for our ride, and it was like a holiday ride in England fifty years ago.' For Lord Lytton he did the same, for the Emerson Tennents, for Mr. Layard and Mr. Helps, for Lady Molesworth and the Higginses (Jacob Omnium), and such other less frequent visitors."

Of the Welcome Home which was given to him after his American reading tour, Dickens tells in a letter to Mrs. Fields, the wife of the American publisher ; it is dated 25th May, 1868 :

As you ask me about the dogs, I begin with them. When I came down first, I came to Gravesend, five miles off. The two Newfoundland dogs, coming to meet me with the usual carriage and the usual driver, and beholding me coming in my usual dress out at the usual door, it struck me that their recollection of my having been absent for any unusual time was at once cancelled. They behaved (they are both young dogs) exactly in their usual manner ; coming behind the basket phaeton as we trotted along, and lifting their heads to have their ears pulled —a special attention which they receive from no one else. But when I drove into the stable-yard, Linda (the St. Bernard) was greatly excited ; weeping profusely, and throwing herself on her back that she might caress my foot with her great fore-paws. Mamie's little dog, too, Mrs. Bouncer, barked in the greatest agitation on being called down and asked by Mamie " Who is this ? " and tore round and round me, like the dog in the Faust outlines. You must know that all the farmers turned out on the road in their market-chaises to say, " Welcome home, sir ! " and that all the houses along the road were dressed with flags ; and that our servants, to cut out the rest, had dressed this house so that every brick of it was hidden. They had asked Mamie's permission to " ring the alarm-bell " (!) when master drove up, but Mamie, having some slight idea that that compliment might awaken master's sense of the ludicrous, had recommended bell abstinence. But on Sunday the village choir (which includes the bell-ringers) made amends. After some unusually brief pious reflections in the crowns of their hats at the end of the sermon, the ringers bolted out and rang like mad until I got home. There had been a conspiracy among the villagers to take the horse out, if I had come to our own station, and draw me here. Mamie and Georgy had got wind of it and warned me.

Of Longfellow's visit to Dickens at Gad's Hill, an account is given in Dickens's letter to James T. Fields, dated 7th July, 1868 :

I have delayed writing to you (and Mrs. Fields, to whom my love) until I should have seen Longfellow. When he was in London the first time he came and went without reporting himself, and left me in a state of unspeakable discomfiture. (Indeed, I should not have believed in his having been here at all, if Mrs. Procter had not told me of his calling to see Procter.) However, on his return he wrote to me from Langham Hotel, and I went up to town to see him, and to make an appointment for his coming here. He, the girls, and Appleton, came down last Saturday night and stayed until Monday forenoon. I showed them all the neighbouring country that could be shown in so short a time, and they finished off with a tour of inspection of the kitchens, pantry, wine-cellar, pickles, sauces, servants' sitting-room, general household stores, and even the Cellar Book, of this illustrious establishment. Forster and Kent (the latter wrote certain verses to Longfellow, which have been published in *The Times*, and which I sent to D . . .) came down for a day, and I hope we all had a really " good time." I turned out a couple of postilions in the old red jacket of the old red royal Dover Road, for our ride ; and it was like a holiday ride in England fifty years ago. Of course we went to look at the old houses in Rochester and the old cathedral, and the old castle, and the house for the six poor travellers who, " not being rogues or proctors, shall have lodging, entertainment, and four pence each."

On 9th April, 1869, Dickens wrote to this same American friend, who was to visit him in the June :

There WILL be borage on the lawn at Gad's. Your heart's desire in that matter, and in the minor particulars of Cobham Park, Rochester Castle and Canterbury, shall be fulfilled, please God. The red jackets shall turn out again upon the turnpike road, and picnics among the cherry orchards and hop gardens, shall be heard of in Kent.

IV

Dickens took a great interest in all around him and was revered by the villagers, almost as a squire ! This is borne out by an account given of some Christmas Sports held in 1866, contained in a letter written by him on Christmas Day :

Footraces for the villagers, come off in my field to-morrow. We have been all hard at work all day, building a course, making countless flags, and I don't know what else. Layard is chief commissioner of the domestic police. The country police predict an immense crowd.

There were between two and three thousand people, Forster tells us ; and somehow, by a magical kind of influence, said Layard, Dickens seemed to have bound every creature present, upon what honour the creature had, to keep order. What was the special means used or the art employed, it might have been difficult to say ; but this was the result. Writing on New Year's Day, Dickens himself described it :

We had made a very pretty course, and taken great pains. Encouraged by the cricket matches experience, I allowed the landlord of the Falstaff to have a drinking-booth on the ground. Not to seem to dictate or distrust, I gave all the prizes (about ten pounds in the aggregate) in money. The great mass of the crowd were labouring men of all kinds, soldiers, sailors, and navvies. They did not, between half-past ten, when we began, and sunset, displace a rope or a

stake ; and they left every barrier and flag as
neat as they found it. There was not a dispute
and there was no drunkenness whatever. I
made them a little speech from the lawn, at the
end of the games, saying that please God we
would do it again next year. They cheered
most lustily and dispersed. The road between
this and Chatham was like a Fair all day ; and
surely it is a fine thing to get such perfect be-
haviour out of a reckless seaport town. Among
other oddities we had A Hurdle Race for
Strangers. One man (he came in second) ran
120 yards and leaped over ten hurdles, in twenty
seconds, *with a pipe in his mouth, and smoking it
all the time.* " If it hadn't been for your pipe,"
I said to him at the winning-post, " you would
have been first." " I beg your pardon, sir,"
he answered, " but if it hadn't been for my pipe,
I should have been nowhere."

The main Dover Road was ever noted for its
tramps, and Dickens described that portion of it
that was close to his house at Gad's Hill, in an article
bearing that title, contributed to *The Uncommercial
Traveller.*

I have my eye upon a piece of Kentish road,
bordered on either side by a wood, and having
on one hand, between the road-dust and the
trees, a skirting patch of grass. Wild flowers
grow in abundance on this spot, and it lies high
and airy, with a distant river stealing steadily
away to the ocean, like a man's life. To gain
the milestone here, which the moss, primroses,
violets, blue-bells, and wild roses, would soon
render illegible but for peering travellers pushing
them aside with their sticks, you must come up
a steep hill, come which way you may. So,

all the tramps with carts or caravans—the Gipsy-tramp, the Show-tramp, the Cheap Jack —find it impossible to resist the temptations of the place, and all turn the horse loose when they come to it, and boil the pot. Bless the place, I love the ashes of the vagabond fires that have scorched its grass ! . . . Here, do I encounter the cart of mats and brooms and baskets—with all thoughts of business given to the evening wind—with the stew made and being served out —with Cheap Jack and Dear Jill striking soft music out of the plates that are rattled like warlike cymbals when put up for auction at fairs and markets. . . . On this hallowed ground has it been my happy privilege (let me whisper it) to behold the White-haired Lady with the pink eyes, eating meatpie with the Giant : while, by the hedge-side, on the box of blankets which I knew contained the snakes, were set forth the cups and saucers and the teapot. It was on an evening in August, that I chanced upon this ravishing spectacle, and I noticed that, whereas the Giant reclined half concealed beneath the overhanging boughs and seemed indifferent to Nature, the white hair of the gracious Lady streamed free in the breath of evening, and her pink eyes found pleasure in the landscape. I heard only a single sentence of her uttering, yet it bespoke a talent for modest repartee. The ill-mannered Giant—accursed be his evil race !—had interrupted the Lady in some remark, and, as I passed that enchanted corner of the wood, she gently reproved him, with the words, " Now, Cobby "—Cobby ! so short a name !—" ain't one fool enough to talk at a time ? "

To the Sir John Falstaff Inn, almost opposite, the article goes on to make this reference :

Within appropriate distance of this magic ground, though not so near it as that the song trolled from tap or bench at door, can invade its woodland silence, is a little hostelry which no man possessed of a penny was ever known to pass in warm weather. Before its entrance, are certain pleasant trimmed limes ; likewise, a cool well, with so musical a bucket-handle that its fall upon the bucket rim will make a horse prick up his ears and neigh, upon the droughty road half a mile off. This is a house of great resort for haymaking tramps and harvest tramps, insomuch that they sit within, drinking their mugs of beer, their relinquished scythes and reaping-hooks glare out of the open windows, as if the whole establishment were a family war-coach of Ancient Britons.

Belonging to the house, but on the opposite side of the road, is a shrubbery known as The Wilderness. Dickens constructed an underground passage from the front lawn of the house to this annexe, and when a few years later Fechter the actor presented him with a Swiss Châlet, he had it erected in this part of the grounds.

It will really be a very pretty thing, and in the summer (supposing it is not blown away in the spring), the upper room will make a charming study.

Indeed, it became his favourite place for work in the summer months, and here the last lines of *Edwin Drood* were written.

After his death the Châlet was presented by the family to Lord Darnley, and it is till to be seen in Cobham Park (see page 54).

V

Charles Dickens died at Gad's Hill on the 9th June, 1870.

Of his last days there, let us quote Forster, for none can tell it so well as he :

" He was out with his dogs for the last time on Monday the 6th of June, when he walked with his letters into Rochester. On Tuesday the 7th, after his daughter Mary had left on a visit to her sister Kate, not finding himself equal to much fatigue, he drove to Cobham Wood with his sister-in-law, there dismissed the carriage, and walked round the park and back. He returned in time to put up in his new conservatory some Chinese lanterns sent from London that afternoon ; and the whole of the evening, he sat with Miss Hogarth in the dining-room that he might see their effect when lighted. More than once he then expressed his satisfaction at having finally abandoned all intention of exchanging Gad's Hill for London ; and this he had done more impressively some days before. While he lived, he said, he should wish his name to be more and more associated with the place ; and he had a notion that when he died he should like to lie in the little grave-yard belonging to the Cathedral at the foot of the Castle wall.

" On the 8th of June he passed all the day writing in the Châlet. He came over for luncheon ; and, much against his usual custom, returned to his desk.

" He was late in leaving the Châlet ; but before dinner, which was ordered at six o'clock with the intention of walking afterwards in the lanes, he wrote some letters, among them one to his friend Mr. Charles Kent appointing to see him in London next day ; and dinner was begun before Miss

Hogarth saw, with alarm, a singular expression of trouble and pain in his face. For an hour, he then told her, he had been very ill; but he wished dinner to go on. These were the only really coherent words uttered by him. They were followed by some, that fell from him disconnectedly, of quite other matters; of an approaching sale at a neighbour's house, of whether Macready's son was with his father at Cheltenham, and of his own intention to go immediately to London; but at these latter he had risen, and his sister-in-law's help alone prevented him from falling where he stood. Her effort then was to get him on the sofa, but after a slight struggle he sank heavily on his left side. ' On the ground ' were the last words he spoke."

At the time of writing, Gad's Hill Place has changed ownership, but we trust that the courtesy extended to the public by the late Colonel Latham, will be continued by the new owner. Every Wednesday afternoon the house was open to the public, who were allowed to see the grounds and shrubbery as well as the Dining-room on the ground floor where Dickens died, and the Library in the front of the house where he worked and where the dummy book-backs on the door were to be seen. This was a quaint idea of Dickens and he went to considerable trouble to invent the titles, among which were :

Lady Godiva on the Horse.
Five Minutes in China (3 vols.).
Hansard's Guide to Refreshing Sleep.
The History of a Short Chancery Suit (21 vols.).
Cat's Lives (9 vols.).
Noah's Arkitecture

4

The privilege, however, of paying one's respects to the last home of so great an Englishman as Dickens, should not be dependent on private generosity. Gad's Hill Place is a National Shrine, and should be in the Nation's hands.

CHAPTER IV

SHORNE, COBHAM AND COOLING

" The fairest spot in the Garden of England."
(The Old Man in *The Pickwick Papers*)

I

THE three villages of Shorne, Cobham, and Cooling are best visited from Gad's Hill. They represent the favourite objectives of Dickens for some of his shorter walks. The two former lie to the south of the Dover Road, whilst Cooling is to the north.

There is a lane by the side of Gad's Hill Place which takes us, in about a mile, into the road running from Strood to Cobham. On reaching this road we bear to the right past the quaint Three Crutches Inn and then skirt the grounds of Cobham Hall on the left. In about a mile and a half, a road turns to the right and this takes us to Shorne, about a mile distant.

A more direct way from Gad's Hill to Shorne is to proceed along the Dover Road in the direction of London for about a mile and then take the first turning on the left, when Shorne is reached in under a mile.

This delightful old-world village was a particular favourite with Dickens. Forster tells us that " for a shorter summer walk, he was not less fond of going round the village of Shorne, and sitting on a hot afternoon in its pretty shaded churchyard " ; and according to the same authority, Dickens had expressed a wish to be buried here in what he described in *Pickwick* as " one of the most peaceful and secluded churchyards in Kent." Although not mentioned by name there is little doubt that it is Shorne Churchyard that Dickens referred to in the story of the Queer Client in *The Pickwick Papers* as the last resting place of Heyling's wife and child.

Beneath a plain grave-stone, in one of the most peaceful and secluded churchyards in Kent, where wild flowers mingle with the grass, and the soft landscape around forms the fairest spot in the garden of England, lie the bones of the young mother and her gentle child.

II

From Shorne we regain the Strood-Cobham road already mentioned, and can either cross Cobham Park by a footpath, or skirt it by the road and so reach the village of Cobham.

Again to quote Forster, " round Cobham, skirting the park and village, and passing the Leather Bottle, famous in the pages of *Pickwick*, was a favourite walk with Dickens. . . . Though Maidstone had also much that attracted him to its neighbourhood, the Cobham neighbourhood was certainly that which he had greatest pleasure in ; and he would have taken oftener than he did the walk through Cobham park and woods, which was the last he enjoyed before life suddenly closed upon him, but that here he did not like his dogs to follow."

In the conclusion of *The Seven Poor Travellers* Dickens tells us :

As for me I was going to walk by Cobham Woods, as far upon my way to London as I fancied.

When I came to the stile and footpath by which
I was to diverge from the main road, I bade
farewell to my last remaining Poor Traveller,
and pursued my way alone. . . . Going through
the woods, the softness of my tread upon the
mossy ground and among the brown leaves
enhanced the Christmas sacredness by which
I felt surrounded. As the whitened stems
environed me, I thought how the Founder of
the time had never raised his benignant hand,
save to bless and heal, except in the case of one
unconscious tree. By Cobham Hall, I came to
the village, and the churchyard where the dead
had been quietly buried, " in the sure and
certain hope " which Christmas time inspired.

This way came the Pickwickians in search of the
love-sick Tracy Tupman, after he discovered the
faithlessness of Rachael Wardle. The letter which
he left with the hostler at the Crown at Muggleton
to be forwarded to Mr. Pickwick at Manor Farm
stated that " any letter addressed to me at the
Leather Bottle, Cobham, Kent, will be forwarded—
supposing I still exist " and consequently the party
sped thither in the hopes of obtaining some news
of him.

At Muggleton they procured a conveyance to
Rochester. By the time they reached the last-
named place, the violence of their grief had
sufficiently abated to admit of their making a
very excellent early dinner ; and having procured the necessary information relative to the
road, the three friends set forward again in the
afternoon to walk to Cobham.

A delightful walk it was : for it was a pleasant
afternoon in June, and their way lay through a
deep and shady wood, cooled by the light wind

which gently rustled the thick foliage, and enlivened by the songs of the birds that perched upon the boughs. The ivy and the moss crept in thick clusters over the old trees, and the soft green turf overspread the ground like a silken mat. They emerged upon an open park, with an ancient hall, displaying the quaint and picturesque architecture of Elizabeth's time. Long vistas of stately oaks and elm trees appeared on every side ; large herds of deer were cropping the fresh grass ; and occasionally a startled hare scoured along the ground, with the speed of the shadows thrown by the light clouds which swept across a sunny landscape like a passing breath of summer.

" If this," said Mr. Pickwick, looking about him, " if this were the place to which all who are troubled with our friend's complaint came, I fancy their old attachment to this world would very soon return."

" I think so too," said Mr. Winkle.

This of course describes Cobham Hall and Park. In the park is preserved the Swiss Châlet presented to Dickens by Fechter the actor. It was given to Earl Darnley by the family on Dickens's death. The Châlet stood in The Wilderness at Gad's Hill, and in it Dickens was busy writing the whole of the day before he died.

" It will really be a very pretty thing," he wrote in January, 1865, " and in the summer (supposing it not to be blown away in the spring), the upper room will make a charming study. It is much higher than we supposed." When erected it became a favourite resort in the summer months, and much of Dickens's work was done there. To an American friend he wrote :

I have put five mirrors in the Châlet where I write and they reflect and refract, in all kinds of ways, the leaves that are quivering at the windows, and the great fields of waving corn, and the sail-dotted river.   My room is up among the branches of the trees and the birds and the butterflies fly in and out, and the green branches shoot in at the open windows, and the lights and shadows of the clouds come and go with the rest of the company.   The scent of the flowers, and indeed of everything that is growing for miles and miles, is most delicious.

In *A Christmas Tree* we find his thoughts reverting to Cobham Hall :

There was the daughter of the first occupier of the picturesque Elizabethan house, so famous in our neighbourhood.   You have heard about her ?   No !   Why, *She* went out one summer evening, at twilight, when she was a beautiful girl, just seventeen years of age, to gather flowers in the garden ;   and presently came running, terrified, into the hall to her father, saying, " Oh, dear father, I have met myself ! " He took her in his arms, and told her it was fancy, but she said " Oh no !   I met myself in the broad walk, and I was pale and gathering withered flowers and I turned my head, and held them up ! "   And that night, she died ;   and a picture of her story was begun, though never finished, and they say it is somewhere in the house to this day, with its face to the wall.

There is also an interesting reference to Cobham Hall in the article entitled " Tramps " in *The Uncommercial Traveller* :

Clock-mending again.   Except for the slight inconvenience of carrying a clock under our arm,

and the monotony of making the bell go, whenever we came to a human habitation, what a
pleasant privilege to give a voice to the dumb
cottage-clock, and set it talking to the cottage
family again. Likewise we foresee great interest
in going round by the park plantations, under
the overhanging boughs (hares, rabbits, part-
ridges, and pheasants, scudding like mad across
and across the chequered ground before us), and
so over the park ladder, and through the wood,
until we came to the Keeper's lodge. Then,
would the Keeper be discoverable at his door, in
a deep nest of leaves, smoking his pipe. Then,
on our accosting him in the way of our trade,
would he call to Mrs. Keeper, respecting " t'ould
clock " in the kitchen. Then, would Mrs.
Keeper ask us into the lodge, and on due
examination we should offer to make a good
job of it for eighteenpence ; which offer, being
accepted, would set us tinkling and chinking
among the chubby awe-struck little Keepers for
an hour and more. So completely to the family's
satisfaction would we achieve our work, that the
Keeper would mention how that there was
something wrong with the bell of the turret
stable-clock up at the Hall, and that if we
thought good of going up to the housekeeper on
the chance of that job too, why he would take
us. Then, should we go, among the branching
oaks and the deep fern, by silent ways of mystery
known to the Keeper, seeing the herd glancing
here and there as we went along, until we came
to the old Hall, solemn and grand. Under the
Terrace Flower Garden, and round by the stables,
would the Keeper take us in, and as we passed
we should observe how spacious and stately the

stables, and how fine the painting of the horses'
names over their stalls, and how solitary all;
the family being in London. . . .

Our task at length accomplished, we should
be taken into an enormous servants' hall, and
there regaled with beef and bread, and powerful
ale. Then, paid freely, we should be at liberty
to go, and should be told by a pointing helper
to keep round over yinder by the blasted ash,
and so straight through the woods, till we should
see the town-lights right afore us. Then,
feeling lonesome, should we desire upon the
whole, that the ash had not been blasted, or
that the helper had had the manners not to
mention it. However, we should keep on, all
right, till suddenly the stable bell would strike
ten in the dolefullest way, quite chilling our
blood, though we had so lately taught him how
to acquit himself. . . . So should we lie that
night at the ancient sign of the Crispin and
Crispanus, and rise early next morning to be
betimes on tramp again.

The Crispin and Crispanus Inn mentioned above
is to be seen in Strood, not far from where the road
from Cobham joins the main Dover Road. Inside,
the visitor is directed to a corner seat, which it is
said was the favourite one of Dickens when he used
to call in to rest on his walks in the neighbourhood.

Mr. Pickwick's opinion of Cobham is endorsed
by all who know it :

"And really," added Mr. Pickwick, after half
an hour's walking had brought them to the
village, "really, for a misanthrope's choice, this
is one of the prettiest and most desirable places
of residence I ever met with."

In this opinion also, both Mr. Winkle and Mr. Snodgrass expressed their concurrence.

At the far end of the village we find the Leather Bottle Inn, a quaint and picturesque hostelry famous the world over for its connection with Pickwick.

Having been directed to the Leathern Bottle, a clean and commodious village ale-house, the three travellers entered, and at once inquired for a gentleman of the name of Tupman.

The parlour where Mr. Tupman was discovered seated at the table, "well covered with a roast fowl, bacon, ale and et ceteras . . . looking as unlike a man who had taken leave of this world as possible," is on the left.

"Show the gentlemen into the parlour, Tom," said the landlady.

A stout country lad opened a door at the end of the passage, and the three friends entered a long, low-roofed room furnished with a large number of high-backed leather-cushioned chairs, of fantastic shapes, and embellished with a great variety of old portraits and roughly-coloured prints of some antiquity.

Opposite the Leather Bottle is the church, famed far and wide for its wonderful brasses. "Finish your dinner," said Mr. Pickwick to Mr. Tupman, "and walk with me ; I want to speak with you alone." And accordingly they sought the church-yard for the purpose. "For half an hour," we are told, "their forms might have been seen pacing the churchyard to and fro, while Mr. Pickwick was engaged in combating his companion's resolution."

Mr. Pickwick prevailed, and Mr. Tupman returned to the fold.

It was at this moment that Mr. Pickwick made that immortal discovery, which has been the pride and boast of his friends, and the envy of every antiquarian in this or any other country. They had passed the door of their inn, and walked a little way down the village, before they recollected the precise spot in which it stood. As they turned back, Mr. Pickwick's eye fell upon a small broken stone, partially buried in the ground, in front of a cottage door. He paused.

" This is very strange," said Mr. Pickwick.

" What is strange ? " inquired Mr. Tupman, staring eagerly at every object near him, but the right one. " God bless me, what's the matter ? "

This last was an ejaculation of irrepressible astonishment, occasioned by seeing Mr. Pickwick, in his enthusiasm for discovery, fall upon his knees before the little stone, and commence wiping the dust off it with his pocket-handker-chief.

" There is an inscription here," said Mr. Pickwick. . . . " This is some very old inscription, existing perhaps long before the ancient alms-houses in this place. It must not be lost."

The exultation and joy of the Pickwickians knew no bounds, when their patience and assiduity, their washing and scraping, were crowned with success. The stone was uneven and broken, and the letters were straggling and irregular, but the following fragment of an inscription was clearly to be deciphered :

+

B I L S T

U M

P S H I

S.M.

A R K

Mr. Pickwick's eyes sparkled with delight, as he sat and gloated over the treasure he had discovered.   He had attained one of the greatest objects of his ambition.

For an account of the great controversy that raged round this discovery the reader is referred to the pages of *Pickwick*, but we must not omit here to record the researches of " the presumptuous and ill-conditioned Blotton " :

Mr. Blotton, with a mean desire to tarnish the lustre of the immortal name of Pickwick, actually undertook a journey to Cobham in person, and on his return, sarcastically observed in an oration at the club, that he had seen the man from whom the stone was purchased ; that the man presumed the stone to be ancient, but solemnly denied the antiquity of the inscription —inasmuch as he represented it to have been rudely carved by himself in an idle mood, and to display letters intended to bear neither more nor less than the simple construction of— " BILL STUMPS, HIS MARK."

Mr. Pickwick referred to the stone as having an old inscription, " existing perhaps long before the ancient alms-houses in this place." These are to be seen at the far side of the church.

In " Titbull's Almshouses " in *The Uncommercial Traveller* there is the following reference to these ancient almshouses :

" How do they pass their lives in this beautiful and peaceful place ? " was the subject of my speculation with a visitor who once accompanied me to a charming rustic retreat for old men and women :   a quaint ancient foundation in a pleasant English country, behind a picturesque church and among rich old convent gardens.

There were but some dozen or so of houses and we agreed that we would talk with the inhabitants as they sat in their groined rooms between the light of their fires and the light shining in at their latticed windows.

In 1840 Dickens, Maclise, and Forster spent two days at Cobham and we should imagine they put up at the Leather Bottle. Forster states that Maclise and himself joined Dickens at Broadstairs, where he was spending his summer holiday " for the pleasure of posting back home by way of his favourite Chatham, Rochester and Cobham, where we passed two agreeable days in revisiting well remembered scenes."

The following year Forster records : " I met him at Rochester at the end of September as arranged ; we passed a day and night there ; a day and night in Cobham and its neighbourhood, sleeping at The Leather Bottle ; and a day and night at Gravesend."

Four years later we find Dickens proposing to Forster a visit to this district to celebrate his birthday. " To Rochester we had accordingly gone," says Forster, " he and Mrs. Dickens, her sister with Maclise and Jerrold and myself, going over the old Castle, Watts' Charity and Chatham fortifications on the Saturday, passing Sunday in Cobham Church and Cobham Park ; having our quarters both days at the Bull Inn made famous in Pickwick ; and thus by indulgence of the desire which was always strongly urgent in him, associating his life with those earliest scenes of his youthful time."

In 1848 we again find him writing from Broadstairs to Forster planning to meet him at Paddock Wood Station, and proposing to return together to London by way of Cobham.

His last visit to Cobham was on the 7th June,

1870, the day before he was seized with his fatal illness. He drove to Cobham Wood with Miss Hogarth, there dismissed the carriage and walked round the park and back to Gad's Hill.

III

Cooling is reached by taking the road opposite Gad's Hill Place bearing to the left past Higham Station, and then by many a pleasant winding lane to the borders of the marshes leading to the mouth of the River Thames. On the border of these marshes, is Cooling, a tiny village almost overshadowed by the fine old castle gateway and the church.

It is generally accepted that at Cooling Dickens placed the blacksmith's forge of Joe Gargery in *Great Expectations*, in spite of the fact that there is now no forge there. That has given the opportunity to ardent Dickensian topographers to find some other place for the opening chapters of the story, and thus we find the rival claims of Cliffe, Higham, and Chalk. The two former are sufficiently well placed to rival Cooling in its honour, but Chalk, although it possessed a forge, is on the main Dover Road and could hardly have been the village where Pip had his home.

It has been pointed out that the church at Lower Higham, about two miles west of Cooling, is more desolately situated than the latter church, and stands actually on the marshes, and would therefore be a more likely place of hiding for an escaped convict.

Cooling is certainly not mentioned by name in the book, and it is only natural to suppose that in describing the lonely church on the marshes Dickens had in mind to give a general description rather than a particular one. But we have Forster's word for it that it was Cooling ; he says : " It is strange as I transcribe the words, with what wonderful vividness they bring back the very spot on which we stood when he said he meant to make it the scene of the opening of his story—Cooling Castle ruins and the desolate Church, lying out among the marshes seven miles from Gad's Hill ! "

In another chapter of his *Life of Dickens* Forster tells us of the walks and haunts of Dickens during his residence at Gad's Hill. " To another drearier churchyard, itself forming part of the marshes beyond the Medway, he often took friends to show them the dozen small tombstones of various sizes adapted to the respective ages of a dozen small children of one family which he made part of his story of *Great Expectations*, though, with the reserves always necessary in copying nature not to overstep her modesty by copying too closely, he makes the number that appalled little Pip not more than half the reality. About the whole of this Cooling churchyard, indeed, and the neighbouring castle ruins, there was a weird strangeness that made it one of his attractive walks in the late year or winter, when from Higham he could get to it across country over the stubble-fields."

Emphasis is given to the connection of Cooling with the haunts of Pip by Dolby in *Charles Dickens as I Knew Him*, when he te ls us of a visit paid to Gad's Hill in the June of 1869, and how the bad weather seldom kept Dickens from his pleasurable pursuit of wa king. " Many a misty wa k we took," writes Do by, " to the marshes at Cooling that we might get a realistic notion of the dreariness and loneliness of the scenes in *Great Expectations*, made

famous by Pip and the convict.   On such occasions
as these we not unfrequently returned wetted to
the skin by a drenching rain."

The opening of *Great Expectations* takes us at
once into the marshlands of this district :

> Ours was the marsh country, down by the
> river, within, as the river wound, twenty miles
> of the sea.   My first most vivid and broad
> impression of the identity of things, seems to
> me to have been gained on a memorable raw
> afternoon towards evening.   At such a time I
> found out for certain, that this bleak place over-
> grown with nettles was the churchyard . . .
> that the dark flat wilderness beyond the church-
> yard, intersected with dykes and mounds and
> gates, with scattered cattle feeding on it, was
> the marshes ; and that the low leaden line
> beyond was the river ; and that the distant
> savage lair from which the wind was rushing,
> was the sea.

The " little stone lozenges " referred to later are
to be seen in the churchyard, and we can easily
conjure up a vision of little Pip playing among them,
and receiving a terrible fright at the unlooked-for
appearance of Magwitch from behind one of the
larger tombstones :

> As I never saw my father or my mother, and
> never saw any likeness of either of them (for
> their days were long before the days of photo-
> graphs) my first fancies regarding what they
> were like, were unreasonably derived from their
> tombstones.   The shape of the letters on my
> father's, gave me an odd idea that he was a
> square, stout, dark man, with curly black hair.
> From the character and turn of the inscription,
> " Also Georgiana Wife of the Above," I drew a

childish conclusion that my mother was freckled and sickly. To five little stone lozenges, each about a foot and a half long, which were arranged in a neat row beside their grave, and were sacred to the memory of five little brothers of mine—who gave up trying to get a living exceedingly early in that universal struggle—I am indebted for a belief I religiously entertained that they had all been born on their backs with their hands in their trousers-pockets, and had never taken them out in this state of existence. In referring to Joe Gargery's forge we read :

Joe's forge adjoined our house, which was a wooden house, as many of the dwellings in our country were—most of them, at that time.

As we have pointed out there is no forge now at Cooling, although the name of the inn The Horseshoe is certainly mindful of one ; but there was a blacksmith's forge there when Dickens knew the place. Dickens may nevertheless have had in mind the forge at Chalk, which was similarly attached to a wooden house.

Of course there was a public-house in the village, and of course Joe liked sometimes to smoke his pipe there. I had received strict orders from my sister to call for him at the Three Jolly Bargemen, that evening, on my way from school, and bring him home at my peril. To the Three Jolly Bargemen, therefore, I directed my steps.

There was a bar at the Jolly Bargemen, with some alarmingly long chalk scores in it on the wall at the side of the door, which seemed to me to be never paid off. They had been there ever since I could remember, and had grown more than I had. But there was a quantity of chalk about our country, and perhaps the people neglected no opportunity of turning it to account.

There is, unfortunately, no such inn as the Three Jolly Bargemen either at Cooling or elsewhere in the neighbourhood ; we must therefore regard it simply as a fancy title.

A battery such as Dickens refers to in connection with the education of Joe, was at the time a conspicuous part of the marshes.

The old Battery out on the marshes was our place of study, and a broken slate and a short piece of slate pencil were our educational implements : to which Joe always added a pipe of tobacco. I never knew Joe to remember anything from one Sunday to another, or to acquire, under my tuition, any piece of information whatever. Yet he would smoke his pipe at the Battery with a far more sagacious air than anywhere else—even with a learned air— as if he considered himself to be advancing immensely.

It was pleasant and quiet, out there with the sails on the river passing beyond the earthwork, and sometimes, when the tide was low, looking as if they belonged to sunken ships that were still sailing on at the bottom of the water.

The " little sluice by the lime kiln " where Pip was decoyed by Orlick and nearly me his death, has not yet been found. It was on the marshes, we are told, but " miles apart " from the Battery.

CHAPTER V

MAIDSTONE, MUGGLETON AND MANOR FARM

" There an't a better spot o' ground in all Kent."
(The hard-headed man with the pippin face,
Pickwick Papers)

I

MAIDSTONE, the county town of Kent, is eight and a half miles from Rochester ; it is on the Folkestone Road—a road parallel with the Dover Road—and thirty-four and a half miles from London.

From Rochester the Maidstone Road leads out of the city past the Vines and Restoration House (see page 132).

The whole neighbourhood was a pure delight to the novelist and he knew it intimately. He frequently referred to it in his letters to friends. " I have discovered," he wrote to one of them, after he had purchased the house at Gad's Hill, " that the seven miles between Maidstone and Rochester is one of the most beautiful roads in England." Ten years before that, whilst on a stay at Broadstairs, he wrote to Forster suggesting a walking excursion on part of his way back from that seaside resort :

> You will come down booked for Maidstone (I will meet you at Paddock Wood) and we will go thither in company over a most beautiful little line of railroad. The eight miles' walk

from Maidstone to Rochester and a visit to the
Druidical altar on the wayside, are charming.
This could be accomplished on the Tuesday ;
and Wednesday we might look about us at
Chatham, coming home by Cobham on Thurs-
day.

He not only knew Maidstone well, but was much
attracted to it. Yet it is curious that he only
refers to the county town once or twice in his novels,
such as in *David Copperfield* and *The Seven Poor
Travellers*, and then little more than by name. He
was to make it the scene of an incident in *Edwin
Drood*, as he told Sir Luke Fildes, but he did not
live to carry out the proposal. It will, however,
probably go down to posterity as the original of
" Muggleton," the scene of the famous cricket
match in *Pickwick*.

When one considers the almost innumerable real
places mentioned in *Pickwick*, it strikes one as
particularly remarkable that three places should
have been given fictitious names—Eatanswill,
Muggleton, and Dingley Dell. A profitable dis-
cussion might well arise, Why did Dickens take this
unusual course ? The only reason we can at present
assign for the fictitious names of Muggleton and
Dingley Dell, is that Dickens was not quite sure
of his ground and preferred to present composite
pictures under assumed names, rather than attempt
an exact description of places with which he was
not absolutely familiar.

We are first introduced to Muggleton as the scene
of the cricket match, when the party from Manor
Farm walk over to witness it.

As their walk, which was not above two miles
long, lay through shady lanes, and sequestered
footpaths, and as their conversation turned

upon the delightful scenery, by which they were on every side surrounded, Mr. Pickwick was almost inclined to regret the expedition they had used, when he found himself in the main street of the town of Muggleton.

The only other claimant to the honour of Muggleton is West Malling ; but Malling is not a corporate town, and its only claim to the distinction appears to be that it was a great place for cricket, and therefore most likely to have been in Dickens's mind when writing the accounts of the great match between the All Muggletonians and the Dingley Dellers.

Although Maidstone had some claim to cricket in Dickens's time, and was a corporate town, its other claim to be considered as Muggleton is that it possessed a jail, and a jail forms part of the story of " The Convict's Return," told at Dingley Dell.

Everybody whose genius has a topographical bent knows perfectly well that Muggleton is a corporate town, with a mayor, burgesses, and freemen ; and anybody who has consulted the freemen to the mayor, or both to the corporation, or all three to Parliament, will learn from thence what they ought to have known before, that Muggleton is an ancient and loyal borough, mingling a zealous advocacy of Christian principles with a devoted attachment to commercial rights ; in demonstration whereof, the mayor, corporation, and other inhabitants, have presented at divers times, no fewer than one thousand four hundred and twenty petitions against the continuance of negro slavery abroad, and an equal number against any interference with the factory system at home ; sixty-eight in favour of the sale of livings in the Church, and eighty-six for abolishing Sunday trading in the street.

Describing the town, Dickens says :

Mr. Pickwick stood in the principal street of this illustrious town, and gazed with an air of curiosity, not unmixed with interest, on the objects around him. There was an open square for the market-place ; and in the centre of it, a large inn with a sign-post in front, displaying an object very common in art, but rarely met with in nature—to wit, a blue lion, with three bow legs in the air, balancing himself on the extreme point of the centre claw of his fourth foot. There were, within sight, an auctioneer's and fire-agency office, a corn-factor's, a linen-draper's, a saddler's, a distiller's, a grocer's, and a shoe-shop—the last mentioned warehouse being also appropriated to the diffusion of hats, bonnets, wearing apparel, cotton umbrellas, and useful knowledge. There was a red brick house with a small paved court-yard in front, which anybody might have known belonged to the attorney ; and there was, moreover, another red brick house with Venetian blinds, and a large brass door-plate, with a very legible announcement that it belonged to the surgeon.

There is very little left of the old Muggleton that one can find in Maidstone to-day ; yet it is a pleasant county town, with a spacious market square, large inns, and many antiquities well worth inspecting.

The Pickwickians made their first acquaintance with Dingley Dell and Muggleton from Rochester. They had been invited by Mr. Wardle, whom they met at Chatham, to spend a few days at Manor Farm.

The waiter at the Bull, Rochester, declared it was
" fifteen miles cross road."

We learn later that Muggleton was " not above
two miles " from Dingley Dell—hence, Muggleton
must be either thirteen or seventeen miles from
Rochester.   Actually Maidstone is eight and a
half miles from Rochester, but Dickens may never
have approached it from Rochester direct until a
much later date.

II

At about the time these early chapters of *Pickwick*
were being written, Dickens was spending his
honeymoon at Chalk near Gravesend.   At that time
the tenant of Cob Tree, Sandling, which is generally
considered as the original of Manor Farm, was a
Mr. William Spong, said to be the prototype of
Mr. Wardle.   He was buried at Aylesford Churchyard, where a tomb to his memory states that he
was " late of Cob Tree, in the Parish of Boxley,
who died November 15th, 1839."   Dickens may
possibly have met him and visited his house, driving
over there from Chalk, which would account, not
only for his giving a fictitious name to the house,
but for the distance of fifteen miles and " cross
road," and the statement made by his daughter
Mamie in *My Father as I recall Him*, and repeated
personally to Mr. Percy Fitzgerald, that one day,
when driving by " the beautiful back road " from
Rochester to Cobham " he showed me the exact
spot where Mr. Winkle called out ' Whoa, I have
dropped my whip.' "

This statement would seem to indicate that
Dickens knew these by-roads very well during his
early married days, whilst he may not have been so

well acquainted with the main road through
Rochester and over Blue Bell Hill to Maidstone,
which, from the direction in which the chaise
appeared in the High Street, in front of the Bull's
coffee room window, has lead more than one to
assume, was the way of their going. However, we
are told that " Mr. Winkle's horse was drifting *up*
the street in a most mysterious manner," so the
" up " must signify towards London, i.e. in the
direction of Cobham—which would occasion the
party in due course to come to Aylesford and
its bridge, where the chaise came to grief; one
obstacle to this assumption being that the bridge
is described as wooden, whereas Aylesford Bridge
is of stone.

The name Manor Farm may possibly have been
taken by Dickens from a farm of that name at
Frindsbury, which also possesses a large pond, but
generally it is accepted that Cob Tree, a house at
Sandling, in the parish of Boxley, midway between
Aylesford and Maidstone, was the original. We
must not, however, lose sight of the fact that
Manor Farm was in all probability a composite
picture, and that we have no reason to suppose
that Dickens had any particular place in his mind.
My friend, Mr. S. J. Rust, a native of Birling, has
brought forward arguments in favour of that village
as the original of Dingley Dell, which are as every
bit convincing as those used in favour of Sandling.
Mr. Hammond Hall, in his instructive book on
Mr. Pickwick's Kent points out that the name
" Dingley " is to be obtained from the endings of
the names of the hamlet and parish, San(d)l(ing),
Box(ley), in which Cob Tree is situated.

The glory of Cob Tree to the Pickwickians' mind
is the Pond and the Kitchen, the latter just the sort

of place for Christmas revels, and the Pond, viewed with the house in the background, just the picture as Phiz depicted for the scene of the skating party.

In no way does the prospect around Cob Tree belie the description of Manor Farm given in Chapter VI.

"Delightful situation this," said Mr. Pickwick.

"There an't a better spot o' ground in all Kent, Sir," said the hard-headed man with the pippin face.

A further description of the surroundings of Manor Farm is supplied in *Pickwick* on the morning after their arrival :

"Pleasant, pleasant country," sighed the enthusiastic gentleman, as he opened his lattice window. "Who could live to gaze from day to day on bricks and slates, who had once felt the influence of a scene like this ? Who could continue to exist, where there are no cows but the cows on the chimney pots ; nothing redolent of Pan but pan-tiles ; no crop but stone crop ? Who could bear to drag out a life in such a spot ? Who I ask could endure it ? " and, having cross-examined solitude after the most approved precedents, at considerable length, Mr. Pickwick thrust his head out of the lattice, and looked around him.

The rich, sweet smell of the hayricks rose to his chamber window ; the hundred perfumes of the little flower-garden beneath scented the air around ; the deep-green meadows shone in the morning dew that glistened on every leaf as it trembled in the gentle air ; and the birds sang as if every sparkling drop were a fountain of inspiration to them.

At the corner of the road from Manor Farm, where

it joins the main Rochester-Maidstone Road is the Running Horse Inn, a name strongly suggestive of the adventure of the Pickwickians in their journey to Dingley Dell. Here turning to the left in the direction of Rochester we ascend Blue Bell Hill and find the ancient monument known as Kits Coity House, in a field on the left.

This was the favourite place of Dickens for a picnic ; the letter to Forster quoted at the commencement of this chapter shows that Dickens was familiar with this spot before he came to live at Gad's Hill, and in the following letter to Captain Morgan, dated 4th December, 1860, this is undoubtedly the " favourite spot " referred to.

We have a touch of most beautiful weather here now, and this country is most beautiful too. I wish I could carry you off to a favourite spot of mine between this and Maidstone, where I often smoke your cigars and think of you. We often take our lunch on a hillside there in the summer, and then I lie down on the grass—a splendid example of laziness—and say, " Now for my Morgan ! "

Forster also tells us in his *Life of Dickens* :

When such friends as Longfellow and his daughters, or Charles Eliot Norton and his wife, came, or when Mr. Fields brought his wife and Professor Lowell's daughter, or when he received other Americans to whom he owed special courtesy, he would compress into infinitely few days an enormous amount of sight-seeing and country enjoyment, castles, cathedrals, and fortified lines, lunches and picnics among cherry orchards and hop gardens, excursions to Canterbury or Maidstone and their beautiful neighbourhoods, Druid-stone and Blue Bell Hill.

In the Christmas story of *The Perils of Certain English Prisoners* there are one or two references to Snorridge Bottom " betwixt Chatham and Maidstone," where the seaman Gills was employed to frighten birds, and where the shepherd, whom he thinks was probably his father, used to give him " so little of his victuals and so much of his staff " that he " ran away from him to be knocked about the world in preference to Snorridge Bottom."

There is no such place as Snorridge Bottom in Kent, but that it existed in Dickens's mind in the neighbourhood of the equally fictitious Dingley Dell there is but little doubt.

The scene of the adventure of Gabriel Grub and the goblins, as told at Manor Farm in *Pickwick*, was " in an old abbey town down in this part of the country," which points to Malling, which possesses an old abbey, as being the place. One of the scenes shown to Gabriel by the King of the Goblins is typical of the Medway valley :

" Show him some more ! " said the king of the goblins.

At these words, the cloud was dispelled, and a rich and beautiful landscape was disclosed to view—there is just such another, to this day, within half a mile of the old abbey town. The sun shone from out the clear blue sky, the water sparkled beneath his rays, and the trees looked greener, and the flowers more gay, beneath his cheering influence. The water rippled on, with a pleasant sound ; the trees rustled in the light wind that murmured among their leaves ; the birds sang upon the boughs ; and the lark carolled on high her welcome to the morning.

Another story connected with Manor Farm was

that given to Mr. Pickwick by the old clergyman, who explained :

> I found it on the death of a friend of mine— a medical man, engaged in our County Lunatic Asylum—among a variety of papers, which I had the option of destroying or preserving, as I thought proper.

The Kent County Asylum, above referred to, is at Barming Heath, not far from Maidstone.

CHAPTER VI

ROCHESTER AND CHATHAM

" The Birthplace of his fancy."
(FORSTER)
" My boyhood's home—Dullborough."
(The Uncommercial Traveller)

I

THERE is no town in Great Britain—perhaps not in all the world—that has so fascinated a writer throughout his whole life as Rochester fascinated Dickens. Although not his actual birthplace, it was, as Forster says, " the birthplace of his fancy " ; and his thoughts always turned to it in his writings.

Dickens was only four years of age when the family came from Portsmouth to live in the adjacent town of Chatham—and, to quote Richard Doubledick in *The Seven Poor Travellers*, " if anybody present knows to a nicety where Rochester ends and Chatham begins, it is more than I do."

Here the family resided for seven years, and Dickens has left more than one record of the mental pictures he made during that time of the city and its people. Here, as his friend and biographer John Forster states, " the most durable of his early impressions were received ; and the associations that were around him when he died, were those which at the outset of his life had affected him most strongly."

There is preserved in the Eastgate House Museum at Rochester a letter written by Dickens in 1865 thanking a correspondent for a book entitled *Curious Visits to Rochester.*   In it he says :

As I peeped about its old corners with interest and wonder when I was a very little child, few people can find a greater charm in that ancient city than I do.

In the preface to the cheap edition of *Nicholas Nickleby* in 1848 we find him writing :

I cannot call to mind, now, how I came to hear about Yorkshire schools when I was a not very robust child, sitting in bye-places, near Rochester Castle, with a head full of Partridge, Strap, Tom Pipes and Sancho Panza ; but I know that my first impressions of them were picked up at that time.

And when the time came for the father to fill a post in London, deep was his grief at parting with the city he had learnt to love so well.   Forster has left us an impression of this based on an actual conversation with Dickens.

" It was the birth-place of his fancy ; and he hardly knew what store he had set by its busy varieties of change and scene, until he saw the falling cloud that was to hide its pictures from him for ever.   The gay bright regiments always going and coming, the continual paradings and firings, the successions of sham sieges and sham defences, the plays got up by his cousin in the hospital, the navy-pay yacht in which he had sailed to Sheerness with his father, and the ships floating out in the Medway, with their far visions of sea—he was to lose them all. He was never to watch the boys at their games any more, or see them sham over again the sham sieges and defences.   He was to be taken away to London inside the stage-coach Commodore ; and Kentish woods and fields, Cobham Park and Hall, Rochester Cathedral and Castle, and all the wonderful romance together, including a red-cheeked baby he had been wildly in love with, were to vanish like a dream."

In *The Uncommercial Traveller* there is a paper contrasting Dickens's early impressions of the town —which he then calls Dullborough Town—with his view of it as a man. To this article we shall make frequent reference, quoting here only the first portion of it :

It lately happened that I found myself rambling about the scenes among which my earliest days were passed ; scenes from which I departed when a child, and which I did not revisit until I was a man. . . . I call my boyhood's home (and I feel like a Tenor in an English Opera when I mention it) Dullborough. Most of us come from Dullborough who come from a country town. As I left Dullborough in the days when there were no railroads in the land, I left it in a stage-coach. Through all the years that have since passed, have I ever lost the smell of the damp straw in which I was packed—like game— and forwarded, carriage paid, to the Cross Keys, Wood-street, Cheapside, London ? There was no other inside passenger, and I consumed my sandwiches in solitude and dreariness, and it rained hard all the way, and I thought life sloppier than I had expected to find it.

II

Rochester figures under its own name in *The Pickwick Papers, David Copperfield,* and *Christmas Stories.* As " Dullborough Town," " Mudfog," and

" Great Winglebury " it appears in *Sketches by Boz*.
In *Great Expectations* it is called " The Market
Town " and referred to as " Up town " and " Our
town," and in *Edwin Drood*, " Cloisterham."

Although Dickens often wrote of Rochester under
a fictitious name, he made no concealment otherwise
that he was referring to the city he loved so dearly.
His earliest reference to Rochester is in " The
Great Winglebury Duel " (*Sketches by Boz*), written
in 1836.

> The little town of Great Winglebury is exactly
> forty-two miles and three quarters from Hyde
> Park Corner. It has a long straggling quiet
> High Street, with a great black and white clock
> at a small red Town Hall, half way up—a market
> place—a cage—an assembly room—a church—
> a bridge—a chapel—a theatre—a library—an
> inn—a pump—and a post office.

In January of the following year he contributed
the first of the *Mudfog Papers* to *Bentley's Miscelleny*, which he was editing, when he found another
name for his much loved city—but hardly a com-
plimentary one ; no doubt he had in mind the
Chatham portion.

> Mudfog is a pleasant town—a remarkably
> pleasant town—situated in a charming hollow by
> the side of a river, from which river, Mudfog
> derives an agreeable scent of pitch, tar, coals,
> and rope yarn, a roving population in oil skin
> hats, a pretty steady influx of drunken bargemen,
> and a great many other maritime advantages.
> There is a good deal of water about Mudfog, and
> yet it is not exactly the sort of town for a watering
> place, either.

In the February number of *Bentley's Miscelleny*
commenced *Oliver Twist*. Readers of that work, as

subsequently printed, are unaware that Mudfog was the place of Oliver's birth ! Yet this is how the story opened in the magazine—to be altered when issued in volume form :

Among other public buildings in the town of Mudfog, it boasts of one which is common to most towns, great or small, to wit, a workhouse.

It is however in *Pickwick* that Rochester first appears under its real name ; and it is *Pickwick* that commenced the romance centred in the city.

Mr. Pickwick and his three companions had resolved to make Rochester their first halting place.

With notebook and telescope Mr. Pickwick descended on the city, and a fund of genuine good humour, perennial in its freshness, was the result, and pilgrimages are made to Rochester, not so much to see its historic castle and ancient cathedral, as to see the places associated with " The Immortal Pickwick " and the other works of his equally immortal creator.

Our introduction to Rochester is in Chapter II, and as follows :

We do not find, from a careful perusal of Mr. Pickwick's notes on the four towns, Strood, Rochester, Chatham, and Brompton, that his impressions of their appearance differ in any material point from those of other travellers who have gone over the same ground. His general description is easily abridged.

" The principal productions of these towns," says Mr. Pickwick, " appear to be soldiers, sailors, Jews, chalk, shrimps, officers, and dock-yard men. The commodities chiefly exposed for sale in the public streets are marine stores, hardbake, apples, flat-fish, and oysters. The

6

streets present a lively and animated appearance, occasioned chiefly by the conviviality of the military. It is truly delightful to a philanthropic mind, to see these gallant men staggering along under the influence of an overflow, both of animal and ardent spirits ; more especially when we remember that the following them about and jesting with them, affords a cheap and innocent amusement for the boy population. Nothing (adds Mr. Pickwick) can exceed their good humour. It was but the day before my arrival that one of them had been most grossly insulted in the house of a publican. The barmaid had positively refused to draw him any more liquor ; in return for which he had (merely in playfulness) drawn his bayonet, and wounded the girl in the shoulder. And yet this fine fellow was the very first to go down to the house next morning, and express his readiness to overlook the matter and forget what had occurred.

" The consumption of tobacco in these towns (continues Mr. Pickwick) must be very great : and the smell which pervades the streets must be exceedingly delicious to those who are extremely fond of smoking. A superficial traveller might object to the dirt which is their leading characteristic ; but to those who view it as an indication of traffic and commercial prosperity, it is truly gratifying."

In *A Christmas Carol* the first of the three spirits takes Scrooge to the place where he was born, and he sees in the distance " A little market town . . . with its bridge, its church and widening river." This was, of course, Rochester.

It was not until 1854 that Rochester again figured to any large extent in the stories he wrote—

although there were casual references to it and Chatham, as we shall show. This time, the house known as Watts's Charity for Six Poor Travellers, was the subject of one of the Christmas numbers, which he entitled *The Seven Poor Travellers*, Dickens himself making the seventh traveller.

It was in the ancient little city of Rochester in Kent, of all the good days in the year, upon a Christmas eve.

In 1860 *Great Expectations* appeared, and the " Market Town " of that book was of course Rochester, near to which he had lately come to reside.

Ten years later came *Edwin Drood*, and his fancy again turned to the cathedral city as the setting for the story ; and he called the city Cloisterham.

For sufficient reasons, which this narrative will itself unfold as it advances, a fictitious name must be bestowed upon the old Cathedral town. Let it stand in these pages as Cloisterham. It was once possibly known to the Druids by another name, and certainly to the Romans by another, and to the Saxons by another, and to the Normans by another ; and a name more or less in the course of many centuries can be of little moment to its dusty chronicles.

An ancient city, Cloisterham, and no meet dwelling-place for any one with hankerings after the noisy world. A monotonous silent city, deriving an earthly flavour throughout from its cathedral crypt, and so abounding in vestiges of monastic graves, that the Cloisterham children grow small salad in the dust of abbots and abbesses, and make dirt-pies of nuns and friars ; while every ploughman in its outlying fields renders to once puissant Lord Treasurers

Archbishops, Bishops, and such-like, the attention which the Ogre in the story-book desired to render to his unbidden visitor, and grinds their bones to make his bread.

A drowsy city, Cloisterham, whose inhabitants seem to suppose, with an inconsistency more strange than rare, that all its changes lie behind it, and that there are no more to come. A queer moral to derive from antiquity, yet older than any traceable antiquity. So silent are the streets of Cloisterham (though prone to echo on the smallest provocation), that of a summer-day the sunblinds of its shops scarce dare to flap in the south wind ; while the sun-browned tramps, who pass along and stare, quicken their limp a little, that they may the sooner get beyond the confines of its oppressive respectability. This is a feat not difficult of achievement, seeing that the streets of Cloisterham city are little more than one narrow street by which you get into it and get out of it ; the rest being mostly disappointing yards with pumps in them and no thoroughfare—exception made of the Cathedral-close, and a paved Quaker settlement, in colour and general conformation very like a Quakeress's bonnet, up in a shady corner.

In a word, a city of another and a bygone time is Cloisterham, with its hoarse cathedral-bell, its hoarse rooks hovering about the Cathedral tower, its hoarser and less distinct rooks in the stalls far beneath. Fragments of old wall, saint's chapel, chapter-house, convent and monastery, have got incongruously or obstructively built into many of its houses and gardens, much as kindred, jumbled notions have become incorporated into many of its citizens' minds.

All things in it are of the past. Even its single pawnbroker takes in no pledges, nor has he for a long time, but offers vainly an unredeemed stock for sale, of which the costlier articles are dim and pale old watches apparently in a slow perspiration, tarnished sugar-tongs with in-effectual legs, and odd volumes of dismal books. The most abundant and the most agreeable evidences of progressing life in Cloisterham are the evidences of vegetable life in many gardens ; even its drooping and despondent little theatre has its poor strip of garden, receiving the foul fiend, when he ducks from its stage into the infernal regions, among scarlet-beans or oyster-shells, according to the season of the year.

When Mr. Honeythunder paid his first visit to Rochester, he was attended by the Minor Canon.

The rough mental notes made in the first five minutes by Mr. Crisparkle would have read thus, verbatim.

He invited Mr. Honeythunder to dinner, with a troubled mind (for the discomfiture of the dear old china shepherdess lay heavy on it), and gave his arm to Helena Landless. Both she and her brother, as they walked all together through the ancient streets, took great delight in what he pointed out of the Cathedral and the Monastery ruin, and wondered—so his notes ran on—much as if they were beautiful barbaric captives brought from some wild tropical dominion. Mr. Honeythunder walked in the middle of the road, shouldering the natives out of his way, and loudly developing a scheme he had, for making a raid on all the unemployed persons in the United Kingdom, laying them every one by the heels in jail, and forcing them, on

pain of prompt extermination, to become
philanthropists.

Another pleasing picture of Cloisterham is to be
found in the nineteenth chapter of *Edwin Drood.*

Cloisterham is so bright and sunny in these
summer days, that the Cathedral and the monas-
tery-ruin show as if their strong walls were
transparent.   A soft glow seems to shine from
within them, rather than upon them from
without, such is their mellowness as they look
forth on the hot corn-fields and the smoking
roads that distantly wind among them.   The
Cloisterham gardens blush with ripening fruit.
Time was when travel-stained pilgrims rode in
clattering parties through the city's welcome
shades ; time is when wayfarers, leading a gipsy
life between haymaking time and harvest, and
looking as if they were just made of the dust of
the earth, so very dusty are they, lounge about
on cool door-steps trying to mend their unmend-
able shoes, or giving them to the city kennels as
a hopeless job, and seeking others in the bundles
that they carry, along with their yet unused
sickles swathed in bands of straw.   At all the
more public pumps there is much cooling of bare
feet, together with much bubbling and gurgling
of drinking with hand to spout on the part of
these Bedouins ; the Cloisterham police meanwhile looking askant from their beats with
suspicion, and manifest impatience that the
intruders should depart from within the civic
bounds, and once more fry themselves on the
simmering high roads.

His last description of Rochester and its Cathedral
is as beautiful as any he ever penned.

A brilliant morning shines on the old city,

Its antiquities and ruins are surpassingly beautiful, with a lusty ivy gleaming in the sun, and the rich trees waving in the balmy air. Changes of glorious light from moving boughs, songs of birds, scents from gardens, woods, and fields—or, rather, from the one great garden of the whole cultivated island in its yielding time—penetrate into the Cathedral, subdue its earthy odour, and preach the Resurrection and the Life. The cold stone tombs of centuries ago grow warm ; and flecks of brightness dart into the sternest marble corners of the building, fluttering there like wings. He was writing this in the Châlet at Gad's Hill (now in Cobham Park, see page 54) on the afternoon of the June day that was his last on earth ; a very few more words and *The Mystery of Edwin Drood* was laid aside for ever, to prove a mystery that is perhaps unsolvable. A few days before he had been seen in Rochester, " peeping about " the nooks and corners he loved so much, and it was thought that this last number would contain other word-pictures of the city ; but no notes remained.

III

In addition to the general description of Chatham and Rochester given in *Pickwick* and quoted on page 81, there is a racy description of the people of Chatham given by Jingle, in the following words :

Queer place—Dock-yard people of upper rank don't know Dock-yard people of lower rank—Dock-yard people of lower rank don't know small gentry—small gentry don't know tradespeople—Commissioner don't know anybody.

It was to the Barracks at Chatham that Joe Willet was sent on enlisting.

The party embarked in a passage-boat bound
for Gravesend, whence they were to proceed on
foot to Chatham ; the wind was in their favour,
and they soon left London behind them, a mere
dark mist—a giant phantom in the air.

And the story of Richard Doubledick in *The Seven
Poor Travellers* also opens at Chatham.

In the year one thousand seven hundred and
ninety nine, a relative of mine came limping
down, on foot, to this town of Chatham. I call
it this town because if anybody present knows
to a nicety where Rochester ends and Chatham
begins, it is more than I do. . . . He was a
poor traveller and . . . came down to Chatham
to enlist.

In the conclusion of the same book we read in
connection with the parting of the Poor Travellers :

While it was yet scarcely daylight, we all came
out into the street together, and there shook
hands. The widow took the little sailor towards
Chatham, where he was to find a steamboat for
Sheerness ; the lawyer, with an extremely
knowing look, went his own way, without com-
mitting himself by announcing his intentions ;
two more struck off by the cathedral and old
castle for Maidstone ; and the book-pedlar
accompanied me over the bridge. As for me,
I was going to walk by Cobham Woods, as far
upon my way to London as I fancied.

Gaffer Hexam and his son Charley had their birth
in Chatham, for we find Dickens writing to Forster
at the time *Our Mutual Friend* was being planned :

I must use somehow the uneducated father in
fustian and the educated boy in spectacles,
Leech and I saw at Chatham.

There are two detached references to Chatham in

Reprinted Pieces—one in " The Begging Letter Writer " and the other in " The Detective Police " —and a more extended reference to Dullborough Town " my boyhood's home " in the chapter on Birthdays."

Forster in his *Life of Dickens* gives an interesting account of a visit paid to Rochester and district on the occasion of Dickens's thirty-fourth birthday.

Shall we go to Rochester to-morrow week (my birthday) if the weather be as it surely must be, better ?

Dickens wrote him, and Forster then tells us :

" To Rochester accordingly we had gone, he and Mrs. Dickens and her sister, with Maclise and Jerrold and myself ; going over the old Castle, Watts's Charity, and Chatham fortifications on the Saturday, passing Sunday in Cobham Church and Cobham Park ; having our quarters both days at the Bull Inn made famous in *Pickwick* ; and thus, by indulgence of the desire which was always strangely urgent in him, associating his new resolve in life with those earliest scenes of his youthful time."

In the concluding remarks to " Dullborough Town " in *The Uncommercial Traveller* Dickens tells us how he interviewed the greengrocer whom he recognized as knowing in former days, and how to a certain extent he endeavoured to impress him ; but all to no avail.

I had no right I reflected, to be angry with the greengrocer for his want of interest ; I was nothing to him ; whereas he was the town, the cathedral, the bridge, the river, my childhood and a large slice of my life to me.

Of his departure at the conclusion of the visit to his boyhood's home, he writes :

When I went alone to the Railway to catch my train at night I was in a more charitable mood with Dullborough than I had been all day ; and yet in my heart I had loved it all day too. Ah! who was I that I should quarrel with the town for being changed to me, when I myself had come back, so changed, to it! All my early readings and early imaginations dated from this place, and I took them away so full of innocent construction and guileless belief, and I brought them back so worn and torn, so much the wiser and so much the worse !

So much for a brief survey of Dickens's association with Rochester and Chatham. We shall now proceed to take a ramble through the two towns, noting all the places of interest figuring in his books and in his life.

CHAPTER VII

ROUND ROCHESTER

*" Is this Cloisterham ? . . . It is . . . and I never was
so glad to see it."*

(Luke Honeythunder in *Edwin Drood*)

I

THE most convenient starting place for the purpose
of a ramble through Rochester and Chatham is
Rochester Bridge. This was the way most of
Dickens's characters approached the Cathedral city.
The railway was not even mentioned until *Edwin
Drood,* in which we read :

In those days there was no railway to Cloister
ham, and Mr. Sapsea said there never would be.
Mr. Sapsea said more ; he said there never
should be. And yet, marvellous to consider,
it has come to pass, in these days, that Express
Trains don't think Cloisterham worth stopping
at, but yell and whirl through it on their larger
errands, casting the dust off their wheels as a
testimony against its insignificance. Some remote fragment of Main Line to somewhere else,
there was, which was going to ruin the Money
Market if it failed, and Church and State if it
succeeded, and (of course), the Constitution,
whether or no ; but even that had already so
unsettled Cloisterham traffic, that the traffic,
deserting the high road, came sneaking in from

an unprecedented part of the country by a back
stable-way, for many years labelled at the corner :
" Beware of the Dog."

Old Rochester Bridge, the one we fancy Dickens
always had in his mind's eye, was replaced by the
present one in 1859 ; the balustrades were used in
the construction of the Esplanade in front of the
Castle and one of them was presented to Dickens,
who placed it on the lawn at Gad's Hill, as the
following letter of 13th June, 1859, informs us :

> One of the balustrades of the destroyed Old
> Rochester Bridge has been (very nicely) pre-
> sented to me by the contractors for the works,
> and has been duly stone masoned and set up on
> the lawn behind the house. I have ordered a
> sun dial for the top of it, and it will be a very good
> object indeed.

The bridge has unfortunately in recent years
undergone a further alteration, rendering it somewhat of an eyesore, and obscuring the view of the
Castle and Cathedral, which was formerly a very
pleasing prospect. It was by the bridge that the
Pickwickians first caught sight of Rochester, its
castle and Cathedral, which called forth the admiration of the Pickwickians " when they first came in
sight of the fine old castle " which probably interrupted the stories of the loquacious stranger,
Alfred Jingle, for we read : " In this strain . . . did
the stranger proceed until they reached Rochester
Bridge, by which time the note books, both of
Mr. Pickwick and Mr. Snodgrass, were completely
filled."

> " Magnificent ruin," said Mr. Augustus Snod-
> grass with all the poetic fervour that distinguished
> him. . . .

> " What a sight for an antiquarian," were the

very words which fell from Mr. Pickwick's mouth, as he applied his telescope to his eye.

"Ah ! Fine place," said the stranger, " glorious pile, frowning walls—tottering arches . . . old cathedral too. . . ."

On a later occasion, it will be remembered, Mr. Pickwick was on the bridge wrapped in contemplation of the scene before him, when he was interrupted by the dismal man who made allusion to drowning being a happiness on such a morning ; at which Mr. Pickwick edged " a little from the balustrade, as the possibility of the dismal man's tipping him over, by way of experiment, occurred to him rather forcibly "—maybe the balustrade presented to him was the identical one which supported Mr. Pickwick's portly frame !

Bright and pleasant was the sky, balmy the air, and beautiful the appearance of every object around, as Mr. Pickwick leant over the balustrades of Rochester Bridge, contemplating nature, and waiting for breakfast. The scene was indeed one which might well have charmed a far less reflective mind, than that to which it was presented.

On the left of the spectator lay the ruined wall, broken in many places, and in some, over-hanging the narrow beach below in rude and heavy masses. Huge knots of sea-weed hung upon the jagged and pointed stones, trembling in every breath of wind ; and the green ivy clung mournfully round the dark and ruined battlements. Behind it rose the ancient castle, its towers roofless, and its massive walls crumbling away, but telling us proudly of its own might and strength, as when, seven hundred years ago, it rang with the clash of arms, or resounded with the noise of feasting and revelry. On either side, the banks of the Medway, covered with corn-fields and pastures, with here and there a windmill, or a distant church, stretched away as far as the eye could see, presenting a rich and varied landscape, rendered more beautiful by the charming shadows which passed swiftly across it, as the thin and half-formed clouds skimmed away in the light of the morning sun. The river, reflecting the clear blue of the sky, glistened and sparkled as it flowed noiselessly on ; and the oars of the fishermen dipped into the water with a clear and liquid sound, as the heavy but picturesque boats glided slowly down the stream.

Little David Copperfield records in Chapter XIII how he crossed Rochester Bridge at the end of the second day of his tramp to Dover.

I got, that Sunday, through three-and-twenty miles on the straight road, though not very easily, for I was new to that kind of toil. I see myself, as evening closes in, coming over the bridge at Rochester, footsore and tired, and eating bread that I had bought for supper. One or two little houses, with the notice, " Lodgings for travellers," hanging out, had tempted me ; but I was afraid of spending the few pence I had, and was even more afraid of the vicious looks of the trampers I had met or overtaken. I sought no shelter, therefore, but the sky.

And Richard Doubledick in *The Seven Poor Travellers* " limped over the bridge here with half a shoe to his dusty foot."

There are one or two other incidents directly connected with Rochester Bridge, which we may mention here. We can see Pip after he had news of his Great Expectations, feeling uncomfortable in his resplendent dress as a gentleman, and being pursued across the bridge by Trabbs's boy.

Words cannot state the amount of aggravation and injury wreaked upon me by Trabbs's boy, when, passing abreast of me, he pulled up his shirt collar, twined his side hair, stuck an arm akimbo and smirked extravagantly by, wriggling his elbows and body and drawling to his attendants. " Don't know yah, don't know yah, 'pon my soul don't know yah ! " The disgrace attendant on his immediately afterwards taking to crowing, and pursuing me across the bridge with crows . . . culminated the disgrace with which I left the town.

The river at Rochester is the Medway, and here came Mr. Micawber when, on the advice of some branches of Mrs. Micawber's family, he turned his attention to coals.

" Mr. Micawber was induced to think, on inquiry, that there might be an opening for a man of his talent in the Medway Coal Trade. Then, as Mr. Micawber very properly said, the first step to be taken clearly was, to come and *see* the Medway. Which we came and saw. I say ' we,' Master Copperfield ; for I never will," said Mrs. Micawber with emotion, " I never will desert Mr. Micawber."

I murmured my admiration and approbation.

" We came," repeated Mrs. Micawber, " and saw the Medway. My opinion of the coal trade on that river, is, that it may require talent, but that it certainly requires capital. Talent, Mr. Micawber has ; capital, Mr. Micawber has not. We saw, I think, the greater part of the Medway ; and that is my individual conclusion."

Being so near to Canterbury, we are further
informed they visited that city too, but strange to
say there is no description of Mr. Micawber's stay
in Rochester.

II

The bridge leads straight into the High Street of
which Dickens says in revisiting " Dulborough
Town, ' " of course, the town had shrunk fearfully.
I had entertained the impression that the High
Street was at least as wide as Regent Street, London.
I 'ound it little better than a lane." " The silent
High Street of Rochester is full of gables with old
beams and timbers carved into strange faces," says
Dickens in *The Seven Poor Travellers*, and in " The
Great Winglebury Duel " he describes it as " a long
straggling, quiet High Street, with a great black and
white clock at a small red Town Hall half way up."

At the commencement of High Street, on the
right is the Crown Hotel, once kept by Wright,
referred to by Jingle on the arrival of the Pickwickians, who asked him if he was stopping at the
Bull Inn.

Here—not I—but you'd better—good house
—nice beds—Wright's next house, dear—very
dear—half-a-crown in the bill if you look at the
waiter—charge you more if you dine at a friend's
than they would if you dined in the coffee-room
—rum fellows—very.

The Crown is also said to be the Crozier of
Edwin Drood, where Mr. Datchery put up on his
first arrival in Cloisterham, but Dickens may have
had in mind the Mitre at Chatham (see page 153).

At about this time a stranger appeared in
Cloisterham ; a white-haired personage, with

black eyebrows. Being buttoned up in a tightish blue surtout, with a buff waistcoat and grey trousers, he had something of a military air; but he announced himself at the Crozier (the orthodox hotel, where he put up with a portmanteau) as an idle dog who lived upon his means; and he farther announced that he had a mind to take a lodging in the picturesque old city for a month or two, with a view of settling down there altogether. Both announcements were made in the coffee-room of the Crozier, to all whom it might or might not concern, by the stranger as he stood with his back to the empty fireplace, waiting for his fried sole, veal cutlet, and pint of sherry. And the waiter (business being chronically slack at the Crozier) represented all whom it might or might not concern, and absorbed the whole of the information.

A few doors past the Crown, on the same side is the Bull. This was the destination of the Pickwickians, for after crossing the bridge " they arrived at the Bull Inn, in the High Street, where the coach stopped." On Mr. Winkle enquiring of Jingle if he stayed there the stranger replied, with this striking advertisement of the hotel, of which the subsequent proprietors have not failed to make use, " Here—not I—but you'd better—good house— nice beds."

In " The Great Winglebury Duel " (*Sketches by Boz*) there is a description of the Bull which is missing from any other of ts references.

The Winglebury Arms in the centre of the High Street, opposite the small building with the big clock, is the principal inn of Great Winglebury.

The house is a large one with a red brick and

7

stone front. A pretty spacious hall, ornamented with evergreen plants, terminates in a perspective view of the bar, and a glass case, in which are displayed a choice variety of delicacies ready for dressing, to catch the eye of the new-comer the moment he enters, and excite his appetite to the highest possible pitch. Opposite doors lead to the " Coffee " and " Commercial " rooms ; and a great, wide rambling staircase, three stairs and a landing—four stairs and another landing —one step and another landing—half-a-dozen stairs and another landing—and so on—conducts to galleries of bedrooms, and labyrinths of sitting-rooms, denominated "private " where you may enjoy yourself, as privately as you can in any place where some bewildered being or other walks into your room every five minutes by mistake, and then walks out again, to open all the doors along the gallery till he finds his own.

The whereabouts and identity of the Blue Lion and Stomach Warmer Inn also at Great Winglebury in the same story are not known.

In *Great Expectations* the Bull figures as the Blue Boar, where Pip's sister, becoming so excited by the twenty-five guineas which he had received from Miss Havisham on being bound 'prentice to Joe, that " nothing would serve her but we must have a dinner out of that windfall, at the Blue Boar," on which occason, Pip tells us :

Rather late in the evening Mr. Wopsle gave us Collins's ode, and threw his blood-stain'd sword in thunder down, with such effect that a waiter came in and said, " The Commercials underneath sent up their compliments, and it wasn't the Tumblers' Arms."

Here too Pip stayed, together with Mr. Jaggers,

in the later days when his expectations warranted him living like a gentleman ; but what a difference in the Boar's demeanour, when it was found that the rich and eccentric Miss Havisham was not the founder of his fortunes !

The tidings of my high fortunes having had a heavy fall, had got down to my native place and its neighbourhood, before I got there. I found the Blue Boar in possession of the intelligence, and I found that it made a great change in the Boar's demeanour. Whereas the Boar had cultivated my good opinion with warm assiduity when I was coming into property, the Boar was exceedingly cool on the subject now that I was going out of property.

It was evening when I arrived, much fatigued by the journey I had so often made so easily. The Boar could not put me into my usual bedroom, which was engaged (probably by some one who had expectations), and could only assign me a very indifferent chamber among the pigeons and post-chaises up the yard. But, I had as sound a sleep in that lodging as in the most superior accommodation the Boar could have given me, and the quality of my dreams was about the same as in the best bedroom.

On the ground floor on the right is the coffee-room, in which the amazed Winkle, wrapped in a travelling shawl and dressing gown, met Dr. Slammer's second and was challenged to the duel. From the coffee-room window Mr. Pickwick beheld the " curious little green box on four wheels with a low place like a wire bin for two behind and an elevated perch for one in front " that was to take them to Dingley Dell.

Mr. Pickwick had made his preliminary

arrangements, and was looking over the coffee-room blinds at the passengers in the street, when the waiter entered, and announced that the chaise was ready—an announcement which the vehicle itself confirmed, by forthwith appearing before the coffee-room blinds aforesaid.

Here in this room we can see again the picture Dickens drew for us of the meeting in *Great Expectations* between Pip and Bentley Drummle.

When we drove up to the Blue Boar after a drizzly ride, whom should I see come out under the gateway toothpick in hand, to look at the coach, but Bentley Drummle !

As he pretended not to see me, I pretended not to see him. It was a very lame pretence on both sides ; the lamer, because we both went into the coffee-room, where he had just finished his breakfast, and where I had ordered mine. It was poisonous to me to see him in the town, for I very well knew why he had come there.

Pretending to read a smeary newspaper long out of date, which had nothing half so legible in its local news, as the foreign matter of coffee, pickles, fish-sauces, gravy, melted butter, and wine, with which it was sprinkled all over, as if it had taken the measles in a highly irregular form, I sat at my table while he stood before the fire. By degrees it became an enormous injury to me that he stood before the fire. And I got up, determined to have my share of it. I had to put my hands behind his legs for the poker when I went up to the fire-place to stir the fire, but still pretended not to know him.

The staircase, on which Jingle insulted Dr. Slammer whilst dressed in Winkle's clothes, leads to the ball-room

"Devil of a mess on the staircase, waiter," said the stranger. "Forms going up—carpenters coming down—lamps, glasses, harps. What's going forward?" "Ball, Sir," said the waiter.

The ball-room remains pretty much as it was when Dickens knew it.

It was a long room, with crimson-covered benches, and wax candles in glass chandeliers. The musicians were securely confined in an elevated den, and quadrilles were being systematically got through by two or three sets of dancers. Two card tables were made up in the adjoining card-room, and two pairs of old ladies, and a corresponding number of stout gentlemen, were executing whist therein.

Bedroom No. 17 is pointed out as being the one "occupied by Mr. Pickwick," and Nos. 13 and 19 as the rooms of Messrs. Tupman and Winkle, these two being inter-communicating, for we are told that "Winkle's bedroom is inside mine," said Mr. Tupman, and this ensured the successful abstraction of the former's dress coat, and its subsequent replacement "without troubling him at all about the matter."

No. 17—Mr. Pickwick's room—Charles Dickens himself occupied more than once. In *The Seven Poor Travellers*, we read how he went back to his inn to give the necessary directions for the turkey and roast beef, and, during the remainder of the day, could settle to nothing for thinking of the Poor Travellers.

When the wind blew hard against the windows, —it was a cold day, with dark gusts of sleet alternating with periods of wild brightness, as if the year were dying fitfully,—I pictured them advancing towards their resting-place along various cold roads, and felt delighted to think how little they foresaw the supper that awaited them. . . .

After the Cathedral bell had struck eight, I could smell a delicious savour of Turkey and roast Beef rising to the window of my adjoining bedroom, which looked down into the inn-yard just where the lights of the kitchen reddened a massive fragment of the Castle Wall. It was high time to make the Wassail now ; therefore I had up the materials (which, together with their proportions and combinations, I must decline to impart, as the only secret of my own I was ever known to keep). and made a glorious jorum. Not in a bowl ; for a bowl anywhere but on a shelf is a low superstition, fraught with cooling and slopping ; but in a brown earthen-ware pitcher, tenderly suffocated, when full, with a coarse cloth. It being now upon the stroke of nine, I set out for Watts's Charity, carrying my brown beauty in my arms. I would trust Ben, the waiter, with untold gold ; but there are strings in the human heart which must never be sounded by another, and drinks that I make myself are those strings in mine.

III

Opposite the Bull is the Town Hall, where Pip was bound an apprentice to his brother-in-law Joe Gargery.

The Justices were sitting in the Town Hall near at hand, and we at once went over to have me bound apprentice to Joe in the Magisterial presence. I say, we went over, but I was

pushed over by Pumblechook, exactly as if I
had that moment picked a pocket or fired a rick ;
indeed, it was the general impression in Court
that I had been taken red-handed ; for, as
Pumblechook shoved me before him through the
crowd, I heard some people say, " What's he
done ? " and others, " He's a young 'un, too, but
looks bad, don't he ? " One person of mild and
benevolent aspect even gave me a tract ornamented with a woodcut of a malevolent young
man fitted up with a perfect sausage-shop of
fetters, and entiteld, To be read in my Cell.

The Hall was a queer place, I thought, with
higher pews in it than a church—and with
people hanging over the pews looking on—and
with mighty Justices (one with a powdered head)
leaning back in chairs, with folded arms, or
taking snuff, or going to sleep, or writing, or
reading the newspapers—and with some shining
black portraits on the walls, which my unartistic
eye regarded as a composition of hardbake and
sticking-plaister. Here, in a corner, my in-
dentures were duly signed and attested, and I
was " bound."

In talking of his re-visit to " Dullborough Town "
Dickens confuses the Town Hall with the Corn
Exchange a short distance beyond, which in *The
Seven Poor Travellers* he describes as

oddly garnished with a queer old clock that
projects over the pavement out of a grave red
brick building, as if Time carried on business
there, and hung out his sign.

The description above referred to is as follows :

There was a public clock in it (the High Street),
which I had supposed to be the finest clock in
the world ; whereas it now turned out to be as

inexpressive, moon-faced and weak a clock as ever I saw. It belonged to a Town Hall. . . . The edifice had appeared to me in those days so glorious a structure that I had set it up in my mind as the model on which the Genie of the Lamp built the Palace for Aladdin. A mean little brick heap, like a demented chapel, with a few yawning persons in leather gaiters, and in the last extremity for something to do, lounging at the door with their hands in their pockets, and calling themselves a Corn Exchange.

On the opposite side of High Street we see a quaintly gabled house surmounting a gateway and leading to the Cathedral Close. This is College Gate, but it is better known through the medium of *Edwin Drood* as Jasper's Gate House, and is so marked by a bronze tablet with the City Arms and the following inscription :

College Gate
formerly called " Cemetery Gate "
and afterwards " Chertsey's Gate "
Jasper's Gate House, " Edwin Drood."

We are first introduced to it in Chapter II of *Edwin Drood* as the place where Jasper lodged.

They all three looked towards an old stone gatehouse crossing the Close, with an arched thoroughfare passing beneath it. Through its latticed window, a fire shines out upon the fast-darkening scene, involving in shadow the pendent masses of ivy and creeper covering the building's front.

When Jasper meets Edwin and Neville Landless and asks them to his " gatehouse " :

" All over, then ! Now, my bachelor gatehouse

is a few yards from here, and the heater is on the fire, and the wine and glasses are on the table, and it is not a stone's throw from Minor Canon Corner. Ned, you are up and away to-morrow. We will carry Mr. Neville in with us, to take a stirrup-cup."

After the interview between Rosa and her guardian at the Nuns' House we are told :

As he held it incumbent upon him to call on Mr. Jasper before leaving Cloisterham, Mr. Grewgious went to the gatehouse, and climbed its postern stair. But Mr. Jasper's door being closed, and presenting on a slip of paper the word " Cathedral," the fact of its being service-time was borne into the mind of Mr. Grewgious. So he descended the stair again.

On two subsequent occasions Dickens likens this quaint piece of architecture to a lighthouse.

One might fancy that the tide of life was stemmed by Mr. Jasper's own gatehouse. The murmur of the tide is heard beyond ; but no wave passes the archway, over which his lamp burns red behind his curtain, as if the building were a Lighthouse. . . .

John Jasper's lamp is kindled, and his light-house is shining when Mr. Datchery returns alone towards it. As mariners on a dangerous voyage, approaching an iron-bound coast, may look along the beams of the warning light to the haven lying beyond it that may never be reached, so Mr. Datchery's wistful gaze is directed to this beacon, and beyond.

Inside the gateway on the left is the house of the verger Tope, with whom the much-discussed Dick Datchery came to lodge. He was introduced to it by the boy Deputy.

The boy led the way, and by and by stopped at some distance from an arched passage, pointing.

" Lookie yonder.   You see that there winder and door ? "

" That's Tope's ? "

" Yer lie ; it ain't.   That's Jarsper's."

" Indeed ? " said Mr. Datchery, with a second look of some interest.

" Yes, and I ain't a-goin' no nearer 'Im, I tell yer."

" Why not ? "

" 'Cos I ain't a-goin' to be lifted off my legs and 'ave my braces bust and be choked ; not if I knows it, and not by 'Im.   Wait till I set a jolly good flint a-flyin' at the back o' 'is jolly old 'ed some day !   Now look t'other side the harch ; not the side where Jarsper's door is ; t'other side."

" I see."

" A little way in, o' that side, there's a low door, down two steps.   That's Topesses with 'is name on a hoval plate."

" Good.   See here," said Mr. Datchery, producing a shilling.   " You owe me half of this."

" Yer lie ; I don't owe yer nothing ; I never seen yer."

" I tell you you owe me half of this, because I have no sixpence in my pocket.   So the next time you meet me you shall do something else for me, to pay me."

" All right, give us 'old."

" What is your name, and where do you live ? "

" Deputy.   Travellers' Twopenny, 'cross the green."

The boy instantly darted off with the shilling,

lest Mr. Datchery should repent, but stopped at a safe distance, on the happy chance of his being uneasy in his mind about it, to goad him with a demon dance expressive of its irrevocability.

Mr. Datchery, taking off his hat to give that shock of white hair of his another shake, seemed quite resigned, and betook himself whither he had been directed.

Mr. Tope's official dwelling, communicating by an upper stair with Mr. Jasper's (hence Mrs. Tope's attendance on that gentleman), was of very modest proportions, and partook of the character of a cool dungeon. Its ancient walls were massive, and its rooms rather seemed to have been dug out of them, than to have been designed beforehand with any reference to them. The main door opened at once on a chamber of no describable shape, with a groined roof, which in its turn opened on another chamber of no describable shape, with another groined roof : their windows small, and in the thickness of the walls. These two chambers, close as to their atmosphere, and swarthy as to their illumination by natural light, were the apartments which Mrs. Tope had so long offered to an unappreciative city. Mr. Datchery, however, was more appreciative. He found that if he sat with the main door open he would enjoy the passing society of all comers to and fro by the gateway, and would have light enough. He found that if Mr. and Mrs. Tope, living overhead, used for their own egress and ingress a little side stair that came plump into the Precincts by a door opening outward, to the surprise and inconvenience of a limited public of pedestrians in a narrow way, he would be alone, as in a

separate residence. He found the rent moderate
and everything as quaintly inconvenient as he
could desire. He agreed, therefore, to take the
lodging then and there, and money down,
possession to be had next evening, on condition
that reference was permitted him to Mr. Jasper
as occupying the gatehouse, of which on the
other side of the gateway, the Verger's hole-in-
the-wall was an appanage or subsidiary part.

When the old Opium Woman, Princess Puffer,
came to Rochester on the track of Jasper, she
watched the High Street between the Cathedral
and Eastgate House, and we read :

Accordingly, that same evening the poor soul
stands in Cloisterham High Street, looking at
the many quaint gables of the Nuns' House, and
getting through the time as she best can until
nine o'clock ; at which hour she has reason to
suppose that the arriving omnibus passengers
may have some interest for her. The friendly
darkness, at that hour, renders it easy for her to
ascertain whether this be so or not ; and it is so,
for the passenger not to be missed twice arrives
among the rest.

" Now let me see what becomes of you. Go
on ! "

An observation addressed to the air, and yet
it might be addressed to the passenger, so com-
pliantly does he go on along the High Street
until he comes to an arched gateway, at which
he unexpectedly vanishes. The poor soul
quickens her pace ; is swift, and close upon
him entering under the gateway ; but only sees
a postern staircase on one side of it, and on the
other side an ancient vaulted room, in which a
large-headed, grey-haired gentleman is writing,

under the odd circumstances of sitting open to the thoroughfare and eyeing all who pass, as if he were toll-taker of the gateway : though the way is free.

This house has a melancholy interest, as the last lines Dickens penned had reference to it.

Mrs. Tope's care has spread a very neat, clean breakfast ready for her lodger. Before sitting down to it, he opens his corner-cupboard door ; takes his bit of chalk from its shelf ; adds one thick line to the score, extending from the top of the cupboard door to the bottom ; and then falls to with an appetite.

IV

The Close of Rochester Cathedral naturally figures very largely in the story of *Edwin Drood*.

Service being over in the old cathedral with the square tower, and the choir scuffling out again, and divers venerable persons of rook-like aspect dispersing, two of these latter retrace their steps, and walk together in the echoing Close.

Not only is the day waning, but the year. The low sun is fiery and yet cold behind the monastery ruin, and the Virginia creeper on the Cathedral wall has showered half its deep-red leaves down on the pavement. There has been rain this afternoon, and a wintry shudder goes among the little pools on the cracked uneven flag-stones, and through the giant elm-trees as they shed a gust of tears. Their fallen leaves lie strewn thickly about. Some of these leaves, in a timid rush, seek sanctuary within the low arched cathedral door.

Edwin and Rosa walked here on the occasion

RICKS COLLEGE
DAVID O. McKAY LRC
REXBURG, ID

of the first suggestion of their engagement being broken off.

The two youthful figures, side by side, but not now arm-in-arm, wander discontentedly about the old Close ; and each sometimes stops and slowly imprints a deeper footstep in the fallen leaves.

Sir Luke Fildes' picture " Under the Trees " depicts a part of the Close.

When at length they really decided to part it was here, after a walk by the river, that they said good-bye to each other :

" My dear Eddy," said Rosa, when they had turned out of the High Street, and had got among the quiet walks in the neighbourhood of the Cathedral and the river : " I want to say something very serious to you. I have been thinking about it for a long, long time." . . .

When they came among the elm-trees by the Cathedral, where they had last sat together, they stopped as by consent, and Rosa raised her face to his, as she had never raised it in the old days ;—for they were old already.

Another description of the Precincts also is given in *Edwin Drood*.

Among those secluded nooks there is very little stir or movement after dark. There is little enough in the high tide of the day, but there is next to none at night. Besides that the cheerfully frequented High Street lies nearly parallel to the spot (the old Cathedral rising between the two), and is the natural channel in which the Cloisterham traffic flows, a certain awful hush pervades the ancient pile, the cloisters, and the churchyard, after dark, which not many people care to encounter. Ask the first hundred citizens of Cloisterham, met at random in the streets at noon, if they believed in Ghosts, they would tell you no ; but put them to choose at night between these eerie Precincts and the thoroughfare of shops, and you would find that ninety-nine declared for the longer round and the more frequented way.

In *Great Expectations* there is also a reference to the Cathedral Close, although no other mention of the Cathedral itself is made in that book.

The best light of the day was gone when I passed along the quiet echoing courts behind the High Street. The nooks of ruin where the old monks had once had their refectories and gardens, and where the strong walls were now pressed into the service of humble sheds and stables, were almost as silent as the old monks in their graves. The cathedral chimes had at once a sadder and a more remote sound to me, as I hurried on avoiding observation, than they had ever had before ; so, the swell of the old organ was borne to my ears like funeral music ; and the rooks, as they hovered about the grey tower and swung in the bare high trees of the priory-garden, seemed to call to me that the place was changed, and that Estella was gone out of it for ever.

V

The first reference to Rochester Cathedral is in *Pickwick* when the Pickwickians and Jingle cross the bridge and view it before them ; and Jingle gives the following terse description :

Old Cathedral too—earthy smell—pilgrims' feet worn away the old steps—little Saxon doors

—confessionals like money-takers' boxes at
theatres—queer customers those monks—Popes,
and Lord Treasurers, and all sorts of old fellows,
with great red faces, and broken noses, turning
up every day—buff jerkins too—match-locks—
Sarcophagus—fine place—old legends too—
strange stories : capital.

Cloisterham was but a thin disguise for Rochester ;
and it was at the Cathedral that Jasper was lay
precentor. The story opens with a vision of the
doped Jasper in the opium den in the East End of
London.

An ancient English Cathedral Tower ? How
can the ancient English Cathedral tower be here !
The well-known massive gray square tower of its
old Cathedral? How can that be here ! There
is no spike of rusty iron in the air, between the
eye and it, from any point of the real prospect.
What is the spike that intervenes, and who has
set it up ? Maybe it is set up by the Sultan's
orders for the impaling of a horde of Turkish
robbers, one by one   It is so, for cymbals clash,
and the Sultan goes by to his palace in long
procession. Ten thousand scimitars flash in the
sunlight, and thrice ten thousand dancing-girls
strew flowers. Then, follow white elephants
caparisoned in countless gorgeous colours, and
infinite in number and attendants. Still the
Cathedral Tower rises in the background, where
it cannot be, and still no writhing figure is on the
grim spike.

And the close of the first chapter introduces us
to Cloisterham.

That same afternoon, the massive gray
square tower of an old Cathedral rises before the
sight of a jaded traveller. The bells are going

for daily vesper service, and he must needs attend it, one would say, from his haste to reach the open Cathedral door. The choir are getting on their sullied white robes, in a hurry, when he arrives among them, gets on his own robe, and falls into the procession filing in to service. Then, the Sacristan locks the iron-barred gates that divide the sanctuary from the chancel, and all of the procession having scuttled into their places, hide their faces; and then the intoned words, " WHEN THE WICKED MAN———" rise among groins of arches and beams of roof, awakening muttered thunder.

When Mr. Grewgious, Rosa's guardian, came down from London to visit her he afterwards sought Jasper at the Cathedral.

And, crossing the Close, paused at the great western folding-door of the Cathedral, which stood open on the fine and bright, though short-lived, afternoon, for the airing of the place.

" Dear me," said Mr. Grewgious, peeping in, " it's like looking down the throat of Old Time."

Old Time heaved a mouldy sigh from tomb and arch and vault; and gloomy shadows began to deepen in corners; and damps began to rise from green patches of stone; and jewels, cast upon the pavement of the nave from stained glass by the declining sun, began to perish. Within the grill-gate of the chancel, up the steps surmounted loomingly by the fast-darkening organ, white robes could be dimly seen, and one feeble voice, rising and falling in a cracked monotonous mutter, could at intervals be faintly heard. In the free outer air, the river, the green pastures and the brown arable lands, the teeming hills and dales, were reddened by the sunset;

8

while the distant little windows in windmills and farm homesteads, shone, patches of bright beaten gold.   In the Cathedral, all became gray, murky, and sepulchral, and the cracked monotonous mutter went on like a dying voice, until the organ and the choir burst forth, and drowned it in a sea of music.   Then, the sea fell, and the dying voice made another feeble effort, and then the sea rose high, and beat its life out, and lashed the roof, and surged among the arches, and pierced the heights of the great tower ; and then the sea was dry, and all was still.

Mr. Sapsea, in showing Mr. Datchery the principal sights of Cloisterham, says :

" This is our Cathedral, sir. The best judges are pleased to admire it, and the best among our townsmen own to being a little vain of it." . . .

Then Mr. Datchery admired the Cathedral, and Mr. Sapsea pointed it out as if he himself had invented and built it : there were a few details indeed of which he did not approve, but those he glossed over, as if the workmen had made mistakes in his absence.

The Crypt and the Tower both play important parts in the mystery that surrounds *Edwin Drood*. In the account of the visit paid to them by Jasper in company with Durdles we are told :

They enter, locking themselves in, descend the rugged steps, and are down in the Crypt.   The lantern is not wanted, for the moonlight strikes in at the groined windows, bare of glass, the broken frames for which cast patterns on the ground.   The heavy pillars which support the roof engender masses of black shade, but between them there are lanes of light.   Up and down these lanes they walk, Durdles discoursing of the

" old uns " he yet counts on disinterring, and s'apping a wall, in which he considers " a whole family on 'em " to be stoned and earthed up, just as if he were a familiar friend of the family. The taciturnity of Durdles is for the time overcome by Mr. Jasper's wicker bottle, which circulates freely ;—in the sense, that is to say, that its contents enter freely into Mr. Durdles's circulation, while Mr. Jasper only rinses his mouth once, and casts forth the rinsing.

They are to ascend the great Tower. On the steps by which they rise to the Cathedral, Durdles pauses for new store of breath. The steps are very dark, but out of the darkness they can see the lanes of light they have traversed. Durdles seats himself upon a step. Mr. Jasper seats himself upon another. The odour from the wicker bottle (which has somehow passed into Durdles's keeping) soon intimates that the cork has been taken out ; but this is not ascertainable through the sense of sight, since neither can descry the other. And yet, in talking, they turn to one another, as though their faces could commune together.

After the severe storm on the night when Edwin disappears we read :

It is then seen that the hands of the Cathedral clock are torn off ; that lead from the roof has been stripped away, rolled up, and blown into the Close ; and that some stones have been displaced upon the summit of the great tower. Christmas morning though it be, it is necessary to send up workmen, to ascertain the extent of the damage done. These, led by Durdles, go aloft.

Inside the Cathedral, underneath the effigy of

Watts, the Philanthropist of Rochester, of which Dickens says in *The Seven Poor Travellers*,

> I had been wandering about the neighbouring Cathedral and had seen the tomb of Richard Watts, with the effigy of worthy Master Richard starting out of it like a ship's figurehead,

is a tablet of brass to the memory of Dickens, bearing this inscription :

CHARLES DICKENS
Born at Portsmouth Seventh of February 1812 Died at Gadshill Place by Rochester Ninth of June 1870 Buried in Westminster Abbey.

———

To connect his memory with the scenes in which his earliest and his latest years were passed and with the associations of Rochester Cathedral and its neighbourhood which extended over all his life This tablet with the sanction of the Dean and Chapter is placed by his Executors.

On the right is the little burial ground where Dickens expressed a desire to be buried, but it was found to be full and the greater claim to Westminster Abbey prevailed.

It bears a tablet, inscribed :

This Ground was originally part of the Castle Moat. Charles Dickens wished to be buried here.

There are two references to the graveyard in *Edwin Drood*, the first when " John Jasper, on his way home through the Close, is brought to a standstill by the spectacle of Stony Durdles, dinner-bundle

and all, leaning his back against the iron railing of
the burial-ground enclosing it from the old cloister-
arches "; and the other,

When Mr. Sapsea has nothing better to do,
towards evening, and finds the contemplation of
his own profundity becoming a little monotonous
in spite of the vastness of the subject, he often
takes an airing in the Cathedral Close and there-
about. He likes to pass the churchyard with a
swelling air of proprietorship, and to encourage in
his breast a sort of benignant-landlord feeling,
in that he has been bountiful towards that
meritorious tenant, Mrs. Sapsea, and has publicly
given her a prize. He likes to see a stray face
or two looking in through the railings, and
perhaps reading his inscription. Should he meet
a stranger coming from the churchyard with a
quick step, he is morally convinced that the
stranger is " with a blush retiring," as monu-
mentally directed.

VI

Beyond the west door of the Cathedral there is a
road which takes us into Minor Canon Row to which
reference is made in the *Seven Poor Travellers*.

As I passed along the High Street, I heard the
Waits at a distance, and struck off to find them.
They were playing near one of the old gates of the
City, at the corner of a wonderfully quaint row
of red-brick tenements, which the clarionet
obligingly informed me were inhabited by the
Minor Canons. They had odd little porches
over the doors, like sounding-boards over old
pulpits ; and I thought I should like to see one
of the Minor Canons come out upon his top step,

and favour us with a little Christmas discourse about the poor scholars of Rochester ; taking for his text the words of his Master relative to the devouring of Widows' houses.

This was the Minor Canon Corner of *Edwin Drood*, where the Rev. Canon Crisparkle lived with his Ma, the " China Shepherdess."

Minor Canon Corner was a quiet place in the shadow of the Cathedral, which the cawing of the rooks, the echoing footsteps of rare passers, the sound of the Cathedral bell, or the roll of the Cathedral organ, seemed to render more quiet than absolute silence. Swaggering fighting men had had their centuries of ramping and raving about Minor Canon Corner, and beaten serfs had had their centuries of drudging and dying there, and powerful monks had had their centuries of being sometimes useful and sometimes harmful there, and behold they were all gone out of Minor Canon Court, and so much the better. Perhaps one of the highest uses of their ever having been there, was, that there might be left behind, that blessed air of tranquillity which pervaded Minor Canon Corner, and that serenely romantic state of the mind—productive for the most part of pity and forbearance—which is engendered by a sorrowful story that is all told, or a pathetic play that is played out.

Red-brick walls harmoniously toned down in colour by time, strong-rooted ivy, latticed windows, panelled rooms, big oaken beams in little places, and stone-walled gardens where annual fruit yet ripened upon monkish trees, were the principal surroundings of pretty old Mrs. Crisparkle and the Reverend Septimus as they sat at breakfast.

The road continued, leaving Minor Canon Row behind us on the left, bears round to the right and ascends Boley Hill, where is situated the one time residence of Richard Watts, called Satis House.

When Queen Elizabeth visited Rochester in 1573, Watts entertained her here, on the last day of her stay. To his expressions of regret at having no better accommodation to offer, the Queen replied " Satis," by which name the house was henceforth known.

It is said that Dickens transferred the name of this house to Restoration House (see page 136) when giving a home to Miss Havisham in *Great Expectations*.

VII

From Boley Hill the Castle grounds are soon reached. Our first introduction to Rochester Castle is in the second chapter of *Pickwick* when the Pickwickians viewed it for the first time from the top of the Commodore coach.

" Magnificent ruin," said Mr. Augustus Snodgrass, with all the poetic fervour that distinguished him, when they came in sight of the fine old Castle.

" What a study for an antiquarian," were the very words which fell from Mr. Pickwick's mouth, as he applied his telescope to his eye.

" Ah, fine place," said the stranger, " glorious pile—frowning walls—tottering arches—dark nooks—crumbling staircases——"

A few hours later, when Winkle received the challenge to the duel with Dr. Slammer we are told :

If the principal tower of Rochester Castle had suddenly walked from its foundation, and stationed itself opposite the coffee-room window,

Mr. Winkle's surprise would have been as nothing compared with the profound astonishment with which he had heard this address.

A further description of the Castle is given in a later chapter of *Pickwick* when Mr. Pickwick surveyed the view from Rochester Bridge. Behind the wall of the river embankment, rose, we are told, the ancient castle, its towers roofless, and its massive walls crumbling away, but telling us proudly of its own might and strength, as when, seven hundred years ago, it rang with the clash of arms, or resounded with the noise of feasting and revelry.

In *The Seven Poor Travellers* is a further description of Rochester Castle.

Sooth to say, he (Time) did an active stroke of work in Rochester, in the old days of the Romans, and the Saxons, and the Normans, and down to the time of King John, when the rugged castle— I will not undertake to say how many hundreds of years old then—was abandoned to the centuries of weather, which have so defaced the dark apertures in its walls, that the ruin looks as if the rooks and daws had picked its eye out.

And prior to the Dinner to the Poor Travellers at Watts's Charity, Dickens tells us :

I took up my hat, and went out, climbed to the top of the Old Castle, and looked over the windy hills that slope down to the Medway, almost believing that I could descry some of my Travellers in the distance.

In Dickens's time, before the present Castle grounds were planned, the Castle was rather inaccessible   the follow ng extract from Forster's *Life of Dickens* refers to a visit Forster, Longfellow, and Dickens paid to Rochester in 1842 :

" One day at Rochester, met by one of those prohibitions which are the wonder of visitors and the shame of Englishmen, we overleapt gates and barriers, and, setting at defiance repeated threats of all the terrors of law coarsely expressed to us by the custodian of the place, explored minutely the castle ruins."

Edwin and Rosa took their last walk together by the river when their engagement was broken off.

Her full heart broke into tears again. He put his arm about her waist, and they walked by the river-side together. . . .

The bright frosty day declined as they walked and spoke together. The sun dipped in the river far behind them, and the old city lay red before them, as their walk drew to a close. The moaning water cast its seaweed duskily at their feet, when they turned to leave its margin ; and the rooks hovered above them with hoarse cries, darker splashes in the darkening air.

And on the night of his disappearance Edwin Drood walked this way after he had met the old Opium Woman in the Vines, and prior to his repairing to his Uncle's gatehouse.

He has another mile or so, to linger out before the dinner-hour ; and, when he walks over the bridge and by the river, the woman's words are in the rising wind, in the angry sky, in the troubled water, in the flickering lights. There is some solemn echo of them even in the Cathedral chime, which strikes a sudden surprise to his heart as he turns in under the archway of the gatehouse.

And so *he* goes up the postern stair.

The athletic Minor Canon of *Edwin Drood*—Mr. Crisparkle, was very familiar with the Castle ruins and the river wall, which was a favourite walk too with Helena Landless, whom he met here on one occasion.

The Cathedral being very cold, he set off for a brisk trot after service ; the trot to end in a charge at his favourite fragment of ruin, which was to be carried by storm, without a pause for breath.

He carried it in a masterly manner, and, not breathed even then, stood looking down upon the river.   The river at Cloisterham is sufficiently near the sea to throw up oftentimes a quantity of seaweed. An unusual quantity had come in with the last tide, and this, and the confusion of the water, and the restless dipping and flapping of the noisy gulls, and an angry light out seaward beyond the brown-sailed barges that were turning black, foreshadowed a stormy night.   In his mind he was contrasting the wild and noisy sea with the quiet harbour of Minor Canon Corner, when Helena and Neville Landless passed below him.   He had had the two together in his thoughts all day, and at once climbed down to speak to them together.   The footing was rough in an uncertain light for any tread save that of a good climber ; but the Minor Canon was as good a climber as most men, and stood beside them before many good climbers would have been half-way down.

" A wild evening, Miss Landless ! Do you not find your usual walk with your brother too exposed and cold for the time of the year ?   Or at all events when the sun is down, and the weather is driving in from the sea ? "

Helena thought not. It was their favourite walk. It was very retired.

" It is very retired," assented Mr. Crisparkle, laying hold of his opportunity straightway, and walking on with them. " It is a place of all others where one can speak without interruption, as I wish to do."

VIII

On the occasion when Canon Crisparkle took " a memorable night walk " after the disappearance of Edwin Drood, " he walked to Cloisterham Weir."

He often did so, and consequently there was nothing remarkable in his footsteps tending that way. But the preoccupation of his mind so hindered him from planning any walk, or taking heed of the objects he passed, that his first consciousness of being near the Weir, was derived from the sound of the falling water close at hand. There is no weir nearer to Rochester than Allington Lock, six miles away.

It was starlight. The Weir was full two miles above the spot to which the young men had repaired to watch the storm. No search had been made up here, for the tide had been running strongly down, at that time of the night of Christmas Eve, and the likeliest places for the discovery of a body, if a fatal accident had happened under such circumstances, all lay— both when the tide ebbed, and when it flowed again—between that spot and the sea. The water came over the Weir, with its usual sound on a cold starlight night, and little could be seen of it ; yet Mr. Crisparkle had a strange idea that something unusual hung about the place.

He got closer to the Weir, and peered at its well-known posts and timbers. Nothing in the least unusual was remotely shadowed forth. But he resolved that he would come back early in the morning.

The Weir ran through his broken sleep, all night, and he was back again at sunrise. It was a bright frosty morning. The whole composition before him, when he stood where he had stood last night, was clearly discernible in its minutest details. He had surveyed it closely for some minutes, and was about to withdraw his eyes, when they were attracted keenly to one spot.

He turned his back upon the Weir, and looked far away at the sky, and at the earth, and then looked again at that one spot. It caught his sight again immediately, and he concentrated his vision upon it. He could not lose it now, though it was but such a speck in the landscape. It fascinated his sight. His hands began plucking off his coat. For it struck him that at that spot—a corner of the Weir—something glistened, which did not move and come over with the glistening water-drops, but remained stationary.

He assured himself of this, he threw off his clothes, he plunged into the icy water, and swam for the spot. Climbing the timbers, he took from them, caught among their interstices by its chain, a gold watch, bearing engraved upon its back E. D.

He brought the watch to the bank, swam to the Weir again, climbed it, and dived off. He knew every hole and corner of all the depths, and dived and dived and dived, until he could bear the cold no more. His notion was, that he would find the body ; he only found a shirt-pin sticking in some mud and ooze.

With these discoveries he returned to Cloisterham, and, taking Neville Landless with him, went straight to the Mayor. Mr. Jasper was sent for, the watch and shirt-pin were identified, Neville was detained, and the wildest frenzy and fatuity of evil report rose against him.

IX

A little beyond Jasper's Gate House, and on the opposite side of the way, is the quaintly gabled Watts's Charity, better known as the House of the Seven Poor Travellers after the Christmas story of that name.

Dickens visited it in company with Wilkie Collins in 1854, and the effect of his account of his visit was to remedy the abuse to which his attention was directed.

Strictly speaking, there were only six Poor Travellers ; but, being a traveller myself, though an idle one, and being withal as poor as I hope to be, I brought the number up to seven. This word of explanation is due at once, for what says the inscription over the quaint old door ?

RICHARD WATTS, ESQUIRE,
by his will dated 22nd August, 1579,
founded this Charity,
for Six Poor Travellers,
who, not being Rogues or Proctors,
May receive gratis for one Night,
Lodging, Entertainment,
and Fourpence each.

It was in the ancient little city of Rochester, in Kent, of all the good days in the year upon a Christmas Eve, that I stood reading this inscription over the quaint old door in question.

I had been wandering about the neighbouring Cathedral, and had seen the tomb of Richard Watts, with the effigy of worthy Master Richard starting out of it like a ship's figure-head ; and I had felt that I could do no less, as I gave the Verger his fee, than inquire the way to Watts's Charity. The way being very short and very plain, I had come prosperously to the inscription and the quaint old door.

" Now," said I to myself, as I looked at the knocker, " I know I am not a Proctor ; I wonder whether I am a Rogue ! "

Upon the whole, I came to the conclusion that I was not a Rogue. So, beginning to regard the establishment as in some sort my property, bequeathed to me and divers co-legatees, share and share alike, by the Worshipful Master Richard Watts, I stepped backward into the road to survey my inheritance.

I found it to be a clean white house, of a staid and venerable air, with the quaint old door already three times mentioned (an arched door), choice little long low lattice-windows, and a roof of three gables. The silent High Street of Rochester is full of gables, with old beams and timbers carved into strange faces. It is oddly garnished with a queer old clock that projects over the pavement out of a grave red-brick building, as if Time carried on business there, and hung out his sign. Sooth to say, he did an active stroke of work in Rochester, in the old days of the Romans, and the Saxons, and the Normans ; and down to the times of King John, when the rugged castle—I will not undertake to say how many hundreds of years old then—was abandoned to the centuries of weather which

have so defaced the dark apertures in its walls,
that the ruin looks as if the rooks and daws had
pecked its eyes out.

I was very well pleased, both with my property
and its situation. While I was yet surveying
it with growing content, I espied, at one of the
upper lattices which stood open, a decent body,
of a wholesome matronly appearance, whose eyes
I caught inquiringly addressed to mine. They
said so plainly, " Do you wish to see the house ? "
that I answered aloud, " Yes, if you please."
And within a minute the old door opened, and I
bent my head, and went down two steps into
the entry.

" This," said the matronly presence, ushering
me into a low room on the right, " is where the
Travellers sit by the fire, and cook what bits of
suppers they buy with their fourpences."

Having seen over the house, Dickens hit upon the
idea of entertaining the Six Poor Travellers that
evening, and himself making a seventh.

It was settled that at nine o'clock that night a
Turkey and a piece of Roast Beef should smoke
upon the board ; and that I, faint and unworthy
minister for once of Master Richard Watts,
should preside as the Christmas-supper host of
the six Poor Travellers.

With this in view he returned to the Bull Hotel,
and from his bedroom " could smell a delicious
savour of Turkey and Roast Beef rising to the
window." Here he " made a glorious jorum " of
Wassail, in a brown pitcher.

On the stroke of nine, he set out for Watts's
Charity carrying his " brown beauty " (the pitcher
of Wassail) in his arms   . . the supper following in
procession.

Myself with the pitcher.
Ben with Beer.
Inattentive Boy with hot plates.
Inattentive Boy with hot plates.
THE TURKEY.
Female carrying sauces to be heated on
the spot.
THE BEEF.
Man with Tray on his head, containing
Vegetables and Sundries.
Volunteer Hostler from Hotel, grinning,
And rendering no assistance.

As we passed along the High-street, comet-
like we left a long trail of fragrance behind us
which, caused the public to stop, sniffing in
wonder. We had previously left at the corner
of the inn-yard a wall-eyed young man connected with the Fly department, and well
accustomed to the sound of a railway whistle,
which Ben always carries in his pocket, whose
instructions were, so soon as he should hear
the whistle blown, to dash into the kitchen, seize
the hot plum-pudding and mince-pies and speed
with them to Watts's Charity, where they would
be received (he was further instructed) by the
sauce-female, who would be provided with brandy
in a blue state of combustion.

All these arrangements were executed in the
most exact and punctual manner. I never saw
a finer turkey, finer beef, or greater prodigality
of sauce and gravy ; and my Travellers did
wonderful justice to everything set before them.
It made my heart rejoice to observe how their
wind and frost hardened faces softened in the
clatter of plates and knives and forks, and
mellowed in the fire and supper heat.

X

A little farther along the High Street, on the same side as Watts's Charity, is a venerable brick edifice known as Eastgate House, which figured in *Edwin Drood* as the Nuns' House, the Seminary for Young Ladies kept by Miss Twinkleton at which Rosa was a pupil.

In the midst of Cloisterham stands the Nuns' House : a venerable brick edifice, whose present appellation is doubtless derived from the legend of its conventual uses. On the trim gate enclosing its old courtyard is a resplendent brass plate flashing forth the legend : " Seminary for Young Ladies. Miss Twinkleton." The house-front is so old and worn and the brass plate is so shining and staring, that the general result has reminded imaginative strangers of a battered old beau with a large modern eye-glass stuck in his blind eye.

Whether the nuns of yore, being of a sub-missive rather than a stiff-necked generation, habitually bent their contemplative heads to avoid collision with the beams in the low ceilings of the many chambers of their House ; whether they sat in its long low windows telling their beads for their mortification, instead of making necklaces of them for their adornment ; whether they were ever walled up alive in odd angles and jutting gables of the building for having some ineradicable leaven of busy mother Nature in them which has kept the fermenting world alive ever since ; these may be matters of interest to its haunting ghosts (if any).

The house is marked with an oblong bronze tablet bearing the City Arms and the following inscription :

9

EASTGATE HOUSE.
Built by the Right Worshipful Sir Peter Buck, 1590.
" Westgate House." *Pickwick Papers.*
" The Nuns House." *Edwin Drood.*

In the porch is another bronze tablet with the City Arms and the following inscription :

EASTGATE HOUSE.
The Nuns House of Charles Dickens's *Edwin Drood.*

Purchased by the Corporation in 1887 in the Mayoralty of Sir William Webb Hayward as a Diamond Jubilee Memorial of Her late Majesty Queen Victoria, opened as a Public Museum by the Right Honourable Earl Stanhope, Lord Lieutenant of the County, and President of the Kent Archaeological Society in the Mayoralty of William John McLellan, J.P., on March 30th, 1903.

One of the rooms is set apart as a Dickens Museum and contains many interesting items.

It is generally thought that Dickens had in mind Eastgate House, Rochester, when writing in *Pickwick* the account of Miss Tomkins's Establishment for Young Ladies at Bury St. Edmunds under the name of Westgate House. Indeed, we have only to stand in front of it to see in action the whole scene of Mr. Pickwick scaling the wall with the aid of Sam Weller prior to entering upon his adventure the other side.

" Over against the Nuns' House " was, we are told, the residence of Mr. Sapsea, auctioneer, " the purest jackass in Cloisterham ; " and there, opposite us, is the pretty collection of gabled houses bearing a tablet connecting them with Dickens.

An Oblong Bronze Tablet bearing the City Arms in colours : and the following wording in gold :

" Mr. Sapsea's House." *Edwin Drood.*
' Pumblechook's Premises." *Great Expectations.*

Mr. Sapsea's premises are in the High Street,
over against the Nuns' House. They are of
about the period of the Nuns' House, irregularly
modernised here and there, as steadily deteriorat-
ing generations found, more and more, that they
preferred air and light to Fever and the Plague.
Over the doorway is a wooden effigy, about half
life-size, representing Mr. Sapsea's father, in a
curly wig and toga, in the act of selling. The
chastity of the idea, and the natural appearance
of the little finger, hammer, and pulpit, have
been much admired.

At one time a carved wooden figure of an
auctioneer such as Dickens describes actually did
grace the doorway.

In Dickens's time too the house was kept by John
Bye Fairbairn, a seedsman, and as the " eminently
convenient and commodious business premises
situated within a hundred miles of High Street,"
of Uncle Pumblechook they actually appeared in
Great Expectations.

Mr. Pumblechook's premises in the High Street
of the market town, were of a peppercorny and
farinaceous character, as the premises of a corn-
chandler and seedsman should be. It appeared
to me that he must be a very happy man indeed,
to have so many little drawers in his shop : and
I wondered when I peeped into one or two on
the lower tiers, and saw the tied-up brown paper
packet inside, whether the flower-seeds and bulbs
ever wanted of a fine day to break out of those
jails, and bloom.

It was in the early morning after my arrival

that I entertained this speculation. On the previous night, I had been sent straight to bed in an attic with a sloping roof, which was so low in the corner where the bedstead was, that I calculated the tiles as being within a foot of my eyebrows. In the same early morning, I discovered a singular affinity between seeds and corduroys. Mr. Pumblechook wore corduroys, and so did his shopman ; and somehow, there was a general air and flavour about the corduroys, so much in the nature of seeds, and a general air and flavour about the seeds, so much in the nature of corduroys, that I hardly knew which was which. The same opportunity served me for noticing that Mr. Pumblechook appeared to conduct his business by looking across the street at the saddler, who appeared to transact *his* business by keeping his eye on the coachmaker, who appeared to get on in life by putting his hands in his pockets and contemplating the baker, who in his turn folded his arms and stared at the grocer, who stood at his door and yawned at the chemist. The watchmaker, always poring over a little desk with a magnifying glass at his eye, and always inspected by a group in smock-frocks poring over him through the glass of his shop-window, seemed to be about the only person in the High-street whose trade engaged his attention.

XI

The first turning on the right after passing Watts's Charity, and between it and Eastgate House, is the Maidstone Road. This was formerly known as Crow Lane. Here on the left, on the site now

occupied by shops, once stood a low public-
house known as The White Duck and later as Kitt's
Lodging House. This is said to have been the
Travellers' Twopenny " 'cross the green," in *Edwin
Drood*. Here the stone-throwing Deputy was
employed.

" I'm man-servant up at the Travellers'
Twopenny in Gas Works Garding," this thing
explains. " All us man-servants at Travellers'
Lodgings is named Deputy. When we're chock
full and the Travellers is all a-bed I come out
for my 'elth."

When Jasper makes his first tour of inspection
with Durdles, he returns in this direction from the
Cathedral Crypt.

They have but to cross what was once the
vineyard, belonging to what was once the
Monastery, to come into the narrow back lane
wherein stands the crazy wooden house of two
low stories currently known as the Travellers'
Twopenny :—a house all warped and distorted,
like the morals of the travellers, with scant
remains of a lattice-work porch over the door,
and also of a rustic fence before its stamped-out
garden ; by reason of the travellers being so
bound to the premises by a tender sentiment
(or so fond of having a fire by the roadside in
the course of the day), that they can never be
persuaded or threatened into departure, without
violently possessing themselves of some wooden
forget-me-not, and bearing it off.

The semblance of an inn is attempted to be
given to this wretched place by fragments of
conventional red curtaining in the windows,
which rags are made muddily transparent in the
night-season by feeble lights of rush or cotton

dip burning dully in the close air of the inside. As Durdles and Jasper come near, they are addressed by an inscribed paper lantern over the door, setting forth the purport of the house.

The vineyard referred to above is a little farther along on the right. It is now a public garden called the Vines, and there is a pleasant walk across it into Minor Canon Row and the Cathedral.

In *Edwin Drood* it is called the Monks' Vineyard.

They go on, presently passing the red windows of the Travellers' Twopenny, and emerging into the clear moonlight of the Monks' Vineyard. This crossed, they come to Minor Canon Corner : of which the greater part lies in shadow until the moon shall rise higher in the sky.

On the evening of his disappearance Edwin wanders in this direction and meets the old Opium Woman, who warns him that Edwin is a threatened name.

He strolls about and about, to pass the time until the dinner hour. It somehow happens that Cloisterham seems reproachful to him to-day.

As dusk draws on, he paces the Monks' Vineyard. He has walked to and fro, full half an hour by the Cathedral chimes, and it has closed in dark, before he becomes quite aware of a woman crouching on the ground near a wicket gate in a corner. The gate commands a cross bye-path, little used in the gloaming ; and the figure must have been there all the time, though he has but gradually and lately made it out.

He strikes into that path, and walks up to the wicket. By the light of a lamp near it, he sees that the woman is of a haggard appearance, and that her weazen chin is resting on her hands,

and that her eyes are staring—with an unwinking
blind sort of steadfastness—before her.

Opposite the Vines Gardens is an ancient house
of striking picturesqueness, known as Restoration
House; but to Dickens readers it is the house of
Miss Havisham, that figures so largely in *Great
Expectations.*

Miss Havisham was " an immensely rich and grim
lady," who, we are told, lived " in a large and
dismal house barricaded against robbers and who
led a life of seclusion." Pip thus made his first
acquaintance with it :

> Within a quarter of an hour we came to Miss
> Havisham's house, which was of old brick, and
> dismal, and had a great many iron bars to it.
> Some of the windows had been walled up ; of
> those that remained, all the lower were rustily
> barred. There was a court-yard in front, and
> that was barred ; so, we had to wait, after
> ringing the bell, until some one should come to
> open it. While we waited at the gate, I peeped
> in (even then Mr. Pumblechook said, " And
> fourteen ? " but I pretended not to hear him),
> and saw that at the side of the house there was a
> large brewery. No brewing was going on in it,
> and none seemed to have gone on for a long
> time.

Estella enlightened him further a few minutes
later, by saying :

> " As to strong beer, there's enough of it
> in the cellars already, to drown the Manor
> House."
> " Is that the name of this house, miss ? "
> " One of its names, boy."
> " It has more than one, then, miss ? "
> " One more. Its other name was Satis ;

which is Greek, or Latin, or Hebrew, or all three
—or all one to me—for enough."

" Enough House ! " said I : " that's a curious
name, miss."

" Yes," she replied ; " but it meant more
than it said. It meant, when it was given, that
whoever had this house, could want nothing else.
They must have been easily satisfied in those
days, I should think."

The name of Satis House was taken by Dickens
from the residence of Watts on Boley Hill, to which
we have already referred on page 119.

A walk in this direction was a great favourite
with Dickens. " He would turn out of Rochester
High Street," says Forster, " through the Vines,
where some old buildings, from one of which called
Restoration House he took Satis House for *Great
Expectations*, had a curious attraction for him."

It is on record that the day before his death he
took this walk and was noticed resting near the
spot, and so attentively engaged in observing the
house that it was thought likely he would introduce
it into the story. The chapter he did write on his
return—the last—had reference to the spot.

In *The Seven Poor Travellers* he tells us how after
entertaining them and leaving for his inn,

as I passed along the High Street, I heard the
Waits at a distance, and struck off to find them.
They were playing near one of the old gates of
the city,

and accompanied them

across an open green called the Vines, and
assisted—in a French sense—at the performance
of two waltzes, two polkas and three Irish
melodies before I thought of my inn any
more.

XII

Rochester High Street has many other memories.
We can recall Alfred Jingle, having received the
invitation of the Pickwickians to dine with them,
marching off from the Bull,

Lifting the pinched-up hat a few inches from
his head, and carelessly replacing it very much
on one side, the stranger, with half the brown
paper parcel sticking out of his pocket, walked
briskly up the yard, and turned into the High
Street.

We can conjure up a picture of that " curious
little green box on four wheels with a low place, like
a wine bin, for two behind, and an elevated perch
for one in front, drawn by an immense brown horse,
displaying great symmetry of bone," drawn up in
front of the Bull; and we can see Mr. Winkle
endeavouring to mount the horse on the wrong side;
and the same horse, when ultimately mounted,
" drifting up the street in the most mysterious
manner, side first, with his head towards one
side of the way and his tail towards the other."
We can see Rosa purchasing the Turkish Delicacy
at " the Lumps of Delight Shop "; we can picture
the shop where Neville Landless bought the knapsack and the heavy walking-stick; and the shop
where Edwin went to have his watch repaired, when
the jeweller told him how Jasper had said, " he had
an inventory in his mind of all the jewellery his
gentlemen relative ever wore." We can see the
old Opium Woman wandering in the High Street,
on the watch for the Omnibus that is to bring
Jasper from the railway station, and having her
interview with Mr. Grewgious there. We can see Pip
in *Great Expectations* visiting Mr. Trabb the tailor,

the open window of whose parlour behind the shop " looked into a prosperous little garden and orchard, and there was a prosperous iron safe let into the wall at the side of the fireplace," and we can picture the collapse of the great but nameless character Trabb's boy, as he was directed by his master to show— Door !

Other tradesmen were alike impressed by Pip's accession to fortune ; and we are told :

Whenever I said anything to that effect it followed that the officiating tradesman ceased to have his attention diverted through the window by the High Street and concentrated his mind on me.

On revisiting " the quiet old town once more," Pip tells us how it was not disagreeable to him to be recognized and stared after.

One or two of the tradespeople even darted out of their shops and went a little way down the street before me, that they might turn . . . and pass me face to face. . . . My position was a distinguished one and I was not at all dissatisfied with it.

But it was Trabb's boy who reduced Pip's pride to ashes, posturing in the High Street before an interested crowd, with his " Don't know yah, 'pon my soul, don't know yah," and following him with it, and similar offensive phrases, along the street and even over the bridge.

XIII

Further along on the right, at the commencement of Star Hill, is the Conservative Club, formerly the Theatre Royal, where Jingle acted.

" Haven't I seen you at the theatre, sir ? "

" Certainly," replied the unabashed stranger.
" He is a strolling actor," said the Lieutenant,
contemptuously ; turning to Dr. Slammer—
" He acts in the piece that the Officers of the
52nd get up at the Rochester Theatre to-morrow
night. You cannot proceed in this affair,
Slammer—impossible ! "

In *Edwin Drood*, we are told :

A new grand comic Christmas pantomime is
to be produced at the Theatre : the latter
heralded by the portrait of Signor Jacksonini the
clown, saying " How do you do to-morrow ? "

In revisiting " Dullborough Town " Dickens
makes the following reference to the Theatre :

To the Theatre, therefore, I repaired for con-
solation. But I found very little, for it was in a
bad and declining way. A dealer in wine and
bottled beer had already squeezed his trade into
the box-office, and the theatrical money was
taken—when it came—in a kind of meat-safe in
the passage. The dealer in wine and bottled
beer must have insinuated himself under the
stage too ; for he announced that he had various
descriptions of alcoholic drinks " in the wood,"
and there was no possible stowage for the wood
anywhere else. Evidently, he was by degrees
eating the establishment away to the core, and
would soon have sole possession of it. It was
To Let, and hopelessly so, for its old purposes ;
and there had been no entertainment within its
walls for a long time except a Panorama ; and
even that had been announced as " pleasingly
instructive," and I know too well the fatal
meaning and the leaden import of those terrible
expressions. No, there was no comfort in the
Theatre. It was mysteriously gone, like my

own youth. Unlike my own youth, it might
be coming back some day ; but there was little
promise of it.

We now arrive at about the spot where Rochester
ends and Chatham begins ; we will not attempt to
define it, preferring to remain in the happy ignorance
of Richard Doubledick, one of the *Seven Poor
Travellers*.

"If anybody . . . knows to a nicety where
Rochester ends and Chatham begins, it is more
than I do."

CHAPTER VIII

ABOUT CHATHAM

" *Rambling about the scenes among which my earliest years were passed.*"

(" Dullborough Town ")

I

At the top of Star Hill, New Road branches off to the left, and we follow its course. To the right are the recreation grounds rented from the military authorities by the Corporation of Chatham. Across the recreation grounds to the right is Fort Pitt, and beyond it a meadow, the scene of the memorable duel that was to have been between Mr. Winkle and Dr. Slammer.

" You know Fort Pitt ? "

" Yes ; I saw it yesterday."

" If you will take the trouble to turn into the field which borders the trench, take the footpath to the left when you arrive at an angle of the fortification, and keep straight on 'till you see me, I will precede you to a secluded place, where the affair can be conducted without fear of interruption."

Fear of interruption, thought Mr. Winkle.

It is easy to follow the course of Mr. Winkle and his second, Mr. Snodgrass. First they " climbed the fence of the first field," now the recreation ground ; then they saw, through the light of the sinking sun, the gentleman in the blue coat, who beckoned to them with his hand. As they passed along by the angle of the trench, Mr. Winkle's feelings were greatly disturbed, " it looked like a co'ossal grave." The secluded field in which Dr. Slammer was waiting is to be found at the back of the Fort.

Leaving Fort Pitt and turning to the left we find ourselves in Ordnance Terrace. Here at No. 11 (then No. 2) Charles Dickens lived from 1817 for about three years. The house bears the following tablet :

In this house
Charles Dickens
lived
1817–1821

Dickens's first school, not reckoning the primary lessons he received at his mother's knee, was near the railway station, not far from Ordnance Terrace. Behind the school was the playing field of many pleasant memories, but also, like many other things, it has gone. Upon revisiting Dullborough Town, rambling about the scenes from which he had departed in a coach as a child, *en route* for the blacking factory, and which he did not revisit, until he was a man—he made the discovery as soon as he had alighted from the S.E.R. engine No. 97, " that the station had swallowed up the playing field."

" It was gone," he continues. " The two beautiful hawthorn trees, the hedge, the turf, and all those buttercups and daisies, had given place to the stoniest of jolting roads ; while beyond the station, an ugly dark monster of a tunnel kept its jaws open as if it had swallowed them and were ravenous for more destruction." He then proceeds to recall his youthful memories.

The coach that had carried me away, was melodiously called Timpson's Blue-Eyed Maid, and belonged to Timpson, at the coach-office up-street ; the locomotive engine that had brought me back, was called severely No. 97, and belonged to S.E.R., and was spitting ashes and hot-water over the blighted ground.

When I had been let out at the platform-door, like a prisoner whom his turnkey grudgingly released, I looked in again over the low wall, at the scene of departed glories. Here, in the hay-making time, had I been delivered from the dungeons of Seringapatam, an immense pile (of haycock), by my countrymen, the victorious British (boy next door and his two cousins), and had been recognised with ecstasy by my affianced one (Miss Green), who had come all the way from England (second house in the terrace) to ransom me, and marry me.

Such was one of the gentle games that the " very small and not-over-particularly-taken-care-of-boy " indulged in and such is one of his earliest memories.

The historic and romantic interest in the game was no doubt supplied by Dickens himself. He was a weak lad and hardly played at marbles or cricket, but to quote Forster, " he had always the belief that this early sickness had brought to himself one inestimable advantage, in the circumstance of his weak health having strongly inclined him to reading."

The early impressions of the neighbours in Ordnance Terrace were transferred to his earliest *Sketches by Boz*. In " Our Parish " the old lady was drawn from a Mrs. Newnham who lived at No. 5 ; and the Half Pay Captain was also a near neighbour.

With the Stroughill family, who lived next door, young Charles was particularly friendly ; George is said to have stood for Steerforth, and Lucy with the Golden Hair was his earliest sweetheart and figured in *The Wreck of the Golden Mary*.

II

Leaving the station we soon find ourselves, by way of Railway Street, in High Street, Chatham, once again. Crossing the road, and continuing straight on down Military Road, we find on our right a street oddly called The Brook. A short way down this street, on the right hand, is a lodging-house—No. 18, St. Mary's Place—bearing a tablet inscribed :

In this house
Charles Dickens
lived
1821–1823

Next door is a factory. No. 18 St. Mary's Place was the next home of Dickens, and the factory next door was at one time a chapel presided over by a young Baptist minister, Mr. William Giles, who kept a school to which young Charles was forthwith sent. A great friendship sprang up between master and pupil, and when, at the age of eleven, his father was called up to London, Charles Dickens had to leave his good master and the old place endeared to him by recollections that clung to him afterwards all his life long. " The night before we came away," he told Forster, " my good master came flitting in among the packing cases to give me Goldsmith's ' Bee ' as a keepsake, which I kept for his sake, and its own, a long time afterwards."

It was at this house that a fresh inmate appeared in the person of James Lamert, the son of Dr. Lamert, a widower who had lately married Dickens's aunt, Mary Allen. Dr. Lamert was attached to the Ordnance Hospital in Chatham and was undoubtedly the original of Dr. Slammer in *Pickwick*. The Dickens family was much attached to the Lamerts, one of the younger children being christened Alfred Lamert Dickens, and it was this James Lamert who later on introduced Charles to the Blacking Warehouse at Hungerford Bridge.

Meanwhile James Lamert, who was some years the senior of Charles, took a very friendly interest in him ; it was he who first introduced Dickens to the Theatre, no doubt the one at Rochester referred to on page 138 ; in addition to this he was the prime mover in amateur theatricals at the Hospital, in which not only Charles but Dr. Lamert himself took part. It was during the residence of the family at the house in The Brook that Dickens wrote a play entitled " Misnar, the Sultan of India," which marked the beginnings of a passion for the stage that was with him all his life.

The end of the year 1822 witnessed the departure of the Dickens family to London ; but Charles did not join them there until the following year, remaining behind with his schoolmaster, Mr. Giles. Looking back on this event, he has recorded it in his sketch of " Dullborough Town."

As I left Dullborough in the days when there were no railroads in the land, he says, I left it in a stage coach. Through all the years that have since passed, have I ever lost the smell of the damp straw in which I was packed—like game—and forwarded, carriage paid, to the Cross Keys, Wood Street, Cheapside, London ?

10

There was no other inside passenger, and I consumed my sandwiches in solitude and dreariness,
and it rained hard all the way, and I thought life
sloppier than I expected to find it. . . . The
coach that had carried me away was melodiously
called Timpson's Blue-Eyed-Maid, and belonged
to Timpson, at the coach office up street.

Forster refers to the coach as being the Commodore, the same coach that took the Pickwickians
to Rochester ; but he may have confused the names.
The Blue Eyed Maid was run by a Chatham
coach proprietor named Simpson from the adjacent
town of Brompton, and was therefore more convenient for the lad than the Commodore from
Rochester.

Dickensians know the great love the novelist had
for Chatham and Rochester ; and his sorrow at
having to leave the place where he had made so many
friends, and had spent the joyous schooltime of his
life, must indeed have been really poignant.   Perhaps he felt the impending cloud of his father's
financial difficulties hanging over him.   Forster
tells us :

" In leaving the place I have often heard him say
he seemed to be leaving . . . everything that had
given his ailing little life its picturesqueness or
sunshine.   It was the birthplace of his fancy ; and
he hardly knew what store he had set by its busy
varieties of change and scene, until he saw the
falling cloud that was to hide its pictures from him
for ever."

In " A Child's Dream of a Star " he refers very
touchingly to these days : " There was once a child
and he strolled about a good deal and thought of
a number of things.   He had a sister who was a
child, too, and his constant companion."

From an upper window on the side of the house, the Church and Churchyard of Saint Mary's are visible, just as described in this charming little story : " There was one clear shining star that used to come out in the sky before the rest, near the church spire, above the graves . . . and every night they watched for it, standing hand in hand at a window."

It was in this Chatham house, too, that he made acquaintance with the books that had so great an influence on his later life, as he told us in *David Copperfield* :

My father had left a small collection of books in a little room upstairs to which I had access (for it adjoined my own), and which nobody else in our house ever troubled. From that blessed little room, *Roderick Random, Peregrine Pickle, Humphrey Clinker, Tom Jones, The Vicar of Wakefield, Don Quixote, Gil Blas,* and *Robinson Crusoe* came out, a glorious host, to keep me company. They kept alive my fancy, and my hope of something beyond that place and time —they, and the *Arabian Nights,* and the *Tales of the Genii*—and did me no harm ; for, whatever harm was in some of them, was not there for me ; *I* knew nothing of it. It is astonishing to me now, how I found time, in the midst of my porings and blunderings over heavier themes, to read those books as I did. It is curious to me how I could ever have consoled myself under my small troubles (which were great troubles to me), by impersonating my favourite characters in them. . . . I have been Tom Jones (a child's Tom Jones, a harmless creature) for a week together. I have sustained my own idea of Roderick Random for a month at a stretch, I verily believe. I had a greedy relish for a few volumes of voyages and travels—I forget what, now—that were on those shelves ; and for days and days I can remember to have gone about my region of our house, armed with the centre-piece out of an old. set of boot-trees ; the perfect realisation of Captain Somebody, of the Royal British Navy, in danger of being beset by savages, and resolved to sell his life at a great price. . . . When I think of it, the picture always rises in my mind, of a summer evening, the boys at play in the churchyard, and I sitting on my bed, reading as if for life. Every barn in the neighbourhood, every stone in the church, and every foot of the churchyard, had some association of its own, in my mind, connected with these books, and stood for some locality made famous in them. I have seen Tom Pipes go climbing up the church-steeple ; I have watched Strap, with the knapsack on his back, stopping to rest himself upon the wicket-gate ; and I *know* that Commodore Trunnion held that club with Mr. Pickle, in the parlour of our little village alehouse.

Indeed, herein lies one of the secrets of Charles Dickens's success. He was an actor before he was an author and lived the parts he afterwards put into stories.

III

Chatham Lines are not far from The Brook, and we soon reach the scene of the " grand review " which Mr. Pickwick witnessed when he lost his hat, and found an acquaintance in the jovial Mr. Wardle and family.

The whole population of Rochester and the adjoining towns rose from their beds at an early hour of the following morning, in a state of the utmost bustle and excitement. A grand review was to take place upon the Lines. The manœuvres of half-a-dozen regiments were to be inspected by the eagle eye of the commander-in-chief ; temporary fortifications had been erected, the citadel was to be attacked and taken, and a mine was to be sprung.

Mr. Pickwick was, as our readers may have gathered from the slight extract we gave from his description of Chatham, an enthusiastic admirer of the army. Nothing could have been more delightful to him—nothing could have harmonised so well with the peculiar feeling of each of his companions—as this sight. Accordingly they were soon a-foot, and walking in the direction of the scene of action, towards which crowds of people were already pouring from a variety of quarters.

The appearance of everything on the Lines denoted that the approaching ceremony was one of the utmost grandeur and importance. There were sentries posted to keep the ground for the troops, and servants on the batteries keeping places for the ladies, and sergeants running to and fro, with vellum-covered books under their arms, and Colonel Bulder, in full military uniform, on horseback, galloping first to one place and then to another, and backing his horse among the people, and prancing, and curvetting, and shouting in a most alarming manner, and making himself very hoarse in the voice, and very red in the face, without any assignable cause or reason whatever.

Years afterwards he revisited Chatham Lines, and gave a fuller description of them.

I took a walk upon these Lines and mused among the fortifications, grassy and innocent enough on the surface at present, but tough subjects at the core. Here I saw the artfullest pits and drawbridges, the slyest batteries in most unexpected angles and turnings, the lowest, deepest-set, beetle-browed little windows down among the stinging nettles at the bottom of the trenches. Steeped in these mysteries, I wandered round the trenches of Fort Pitt, and away to Fort Clarence, and looking down the river from the sloping bank I saw even there upon the shore a stranded little fort, with its weather-beaten brick face staring at the mud, which I somehow settled in my mind somehow communicated with all the other forts and had unknown means of blowing them up into the air, if need should be.

The fortifications above mentioned are now obsolete.

Forster tells us that one of the favourite walks of Dickens when he came to live at Gad's Hill was " by Rochester and the Medway, to the Chatham Lines. He would turn out of Rochester High Street through the Vines (where some old buildings, from one of which called Restoration House he took Satis House for *Great Expectations*, had a curious attraction for him), would pass round by Fort Pitt, and coming back by Frindsbury would bring himself by some cross fields again into the high-road."

Chatham Lines was a favourite with him even earlier than this, for in December, 1852, we find him writing to Frank Stone :

Every appearance of brightness ! Shall I expect you to-morrow morning ?   If so, at what hour ? I think of taking train afterwards, and going down for a walk on Chatham Lines.   If you can spare he day for fresh air and an impromptu bit of fish and chop, I can recommend you one of the most delightful of men for a companion. O, he is indeed refreshing ! ! !

On the second night of his walk to Dover, David rested at Chatham, by the fortifications of Fort Pitt.

I sought no shelter therefore but the sky and toiling into Chatham,—which, in that night's aspect, is a mere dream of chalk, and draw-bridges, and mastless ships in a muddy river, roofed like Noah's arks,—crept, at last, upon a sort of grass-grown battery overhanging a lane, where a sentry was walking to and fro.   Here I lay down, near a cannon ; and, happy in the society of the sentry's footsteps, . . . slept soundly until morning.

It was at Chatham that he decided to sell his jacket.

Accordingly, I took the jacket off, that I might learn to do without it ; and carrying it under my arm, began a tour of inspection of the various slop-shops.

It was a likely place to sell a jacket in ; for the dealers in second-hand clothes were numerous, and were, generally speaking, on the look-out for customers at their shop-doors. But, as most of them had, hanging up among their stock, an officer's coat or two, epaulettes and all, I was rendered timid by the costly nature of their dealings, and walked about for a long time without offering my merchandise to any one.

This modesty of mine directed my attention to the marine-store shops, and such shops as Mr. Dolloby's, in preference to the regular dealers. At last I found one that I thought looked promising, at the corner of a dirty lane, ending in an enclosure full of stinging-nettles, against the palings of which some second-hand sailors' clothes, that seemed to have overflowed the shop, were fluttering among some cots, and rusty guns, and oilskin hats, and certain trays full of so many old rusty keys of so many sizes that they seemed various enough to open all the doors in the world.

Into this shop, which was low and small, and which was darkened rather than lighted by a little window, overhung with clothes, and was descended into by some steps, I went with a palpitating heart ; which was not relieved when an ugly old man, with the lower part of his face all covered with a stubbly grey beard, rushed out of a dirty den behind it, and seized me by the hair of my head. He was a dreadful old man to look at, in a filthy flannel waistcoat, and smelling terribly of rum. His bedstead, covered with a tumbled and ragged piece of patchwork, was in the den he had come from, where another little window showed a prospect of more stinging-nettles, and a lame donkey.

This of course was the man who, with his " eyes and limbs," " lungs and liver," " Ah goroo goroo," bid him " go fer fourpence ! "

In a later journey under happier auspices we read :

When we clattered through the narrow street of Chatham, and I caught a glimpse, in passing, of the lane where the old monster lived who had

bought my jacket, I stretched my neck eagerly to
look for the place where I had sat, in the sun
and in the shade, waiting for my money.

IV

In *A Tale of Two Cities*, Charles Darnay is
accused of treason, and in the charge it is alleged
that he went down in the Dover Mail, " got out of
the mail in the night, as a blind, at a place where
he did not remain, but from which he travelled back
some dozen miles or more, to a garrison-dockyard,
and there collected information ; a witness was
called to identify him as having been at the precise
time required, in the coffee room of an hotel in that
garrison and dockyard town, waiting for another
person."

The Dockyard was of course that at Chatham
and the hotel was probably the Mitre in the High
Street, which has a personal assocation with the
boyhood of Dickens.   In the days when the Dickens
family lived at Chatham the landlord of the Mitre
was John Tribe and the two families were on
visiting terms, and young Charles and his sister
Fanny used to sing duets at parties held here.

In " The Holly Tree " is a distinct reference to
the Mitre.

There was an Inn in the cathedral town
where I went to school, which had pleasanter
recollections about it than any of these. . . .
It was the Inn where friends used to put up,
and where we used to go to see parents, and to
have salmon and fowls, and be tipped.   It had
an ecclesiastical sign,—the Mitre,—and a bar
that seemed to be the next best thing to a
bishopric, it was so snug.   I loved the land-

lord's youngest daughter to distraction,—but let
that pass. It was in this Inn that I was cried
over by my rosy little sister, because I had
acquired a black eye in a fight. And though
she had been, that Holly-Tree night, for many
a long year where all tears are dried, the Mitre
softened me yet ;

and there is a further reference to it in *Great
Expectations* when Pip tells us that,

avoiding the Blue Boar, I put up at an inn of
minor reputation down the town, and ordered
some dinner. While it was preparing, I went to
Satis House and inquired for Miss Havisham ;
she was still very ill, though considered something better.

My inn had once been a part of an ancient
ecclesiastical house, and I dined in a little
octagonal common-room, like a font.

It is probable, too, that Dickens had the Mitre
in view when he referred to the Crozier in *Edwin
Drood*, although by many it is thought he referred
to the Crown in Rochester (see page 96).

Nearly opposite the Mitre stood the Mechanics'
Institute, in aid of the funds of which Dickens gave
a reading from his works prior to commencing his
public readings, and several at later dates.

In " Dullborough Town " he thus refers to the
Institute—which was not there in his young days,
having been built in 1858 :

As the town was placarded with references
to the Dullborough Mechanics' Institution, I
thought I would go and look at that establishment next. There had been no such thing in
the town, in my young day, and it occurred to
me that its extreme prosperity might have
brought adversity upon the Drama. I found

the Institution with some difficulty, and should
scarcely have known that I had found it if I had
judged from its external appearance only ; but
this was attributable to its never having been
finished, and having no front : consequently
it led a modest and retired existence up a stable-
yard. It was (as I learnt, on inquiry) a most
flourishing Institution, and of the highest benefit
to the town : two triumphs which I was glad to
understand were not at all impaired by the
seeming drawbacks that no mechanics belonged
to it, and that it was steeped in debt to the
chimney-pots. It had a large room, which was
approached by an infirm step-ladder : the
builder having declined to construct the intended
staircase, without a present payment in cash,
which Dullborough (though profoundly appreciative of the Institution) seemed unaccountably
bashful about subscribing. The large room had
cost—or would, when paid for—five hundred
pounds ; and it had more mortar in it and more
echoes, than one might have expected to get
for the money. It was fitted up with a platform,
and the usual lecturing tools, including a large
black board of a menacing appearance. On
referring to lists of the courses of lectures that
had been given in this thriving Hall, I fancied
I detected a shyness in admitting that human
nature when at leisure has any desire whatever
to be relieved and diverted ; and a furtive
sliding in of any poor make-weight piece of
amusement, shamefacedly and edgewise. Thus,
I observed that it was necessary for the members
to be knocked on the head with Gas, Air, Water,
Food, the Solar System, the Geological periods,
Criticism on Milton, the Steam-engine, John

Bunyan, and Arrow-Headed Inscriptions, before they might be tickled by those unaccountable choristers, the negro singers in the court costume of the reign of George the Second. Likewise, that they must be stunned by a weighty inquiry whether there was internal evidence in Shakespeare's works, to prove that his uncle by the mother's side lived for some years at Stoke Newington, before they were brought to by a Miscellaneous Concert. But, indeed the masking of entertainment, and pretending it was something else—as people mask bedsteads when they are obliged to have them in sitting-rooms, and make believe that they are book-cases, sofas, chests of drawers, anything rather than bedsteads—was manifest even in the pretence of dreariness that the unfortunate entertainers themselves felt obliged in decency to put forth when they came here.

At the foot of Chatham Hill formerly stood an old inn called the Malt Shovel, whose sign bore the rhyme attributed to the Pegasus's Arms in Chapter VI of *Hard Times* :

> " Good malt makes good beer,
> Walk in, and they'll draw it here ;
> Good wine makes good brandy,
> Give us a call and you'll find it handy."

Of the Thames and the Medway at Chatham, Dickens makes some interesting personal remarks at the opening of a paper on " Chatham Dockyard " in *The Uncommercial Traveller*.

> There are some small out-of-the-way landing-places on the Thames and the Medway, where I do much of my summer idling. Running water is favourable to day-dreams, and a strong tidal river is the best of running water for mine.

I like to watch the great ships standing out to sea or coming home richly laden, the active little steam-tugs confidently puffing with them to and from the sea-horizon, the fleet of barges that seem to have plucked their brown and russet sails from the ripe trees in the landscape, the heavy old colliers, light in ballast, floundering down before the tide, the light screw barks and schooners imperiously holding a straight course while the others patiently tack and go about, the yachts with their tiny hulls and great white sheets of canvas, the little sailing-boats bobbing to and fro on their errands of pleasure or business and—as it is the nature of little people to do—making a prodigious fuss about their small affairs. Then follows what is intended to be a vision of himself as a boy at Chatham.

One of these landing-places is near an old fort (I can see the Nore Light from it with my pocket-glass), from which fort mysteriously emerges a boy, to whom I am much indebted for additions to my scanty stock of knowledge. He is a young boy, with an intelligent face burnt to a dust colour by the summer sun, and with crisp hair of the same hue. He is a boy in whom I have perceived nothing incompatible with habits of studious inquiry and meditation, unless an evanescent black eye (I was delicate of inquiring how occasioned) should be so considered. To him am I indebted for ability to identify a Custom-house boat at any distance, and for acquaintance with all the forms and ceremonies observed by a homeward-bound Indiaman coming up the river, when the Custom-house officers go aboard her. But for him, I might never have heard of " the dumb-ague,"

respecting which malady I am now learned.
Had I never sat at his feet, I might have finished
my mortal career and never known that when
I see a white horse on a barge's sail, that barge
is a lime barge. For precious secrets in reference
to beer, am I likewise beholden to him, involving
warning against the beer of a certain establishment, by reason of its having turned sour
through failure in point of demand : though my
young sage is not of opinion that similar
deterioration has befallen the ale. He has also
enlightened me touching the mushrooms of the
marshes, and has gently reproved my ignorance
in having supposed them to be impregnated
with salt.

Chatham Dockyard, he tells us,

resounded with the noise of hammers beating
upon iron ; and the great sheds or slips under
which the mighty men-of-war are built, loomed
business-like when contemplated from the
opposite side of the river. For all that, however,
the Yard made no display, but kept itself snug
under hill-sides of corn-fields, hop-gardens, and
orchards ; its great chimneys smoking with a
quiet—almost a lazy—air, like giants smoking
tobacco ; and the great Shears moored off it,
looking meekly and inoffensively out of pro-
portion, like the Giraffe of the machinery
creation. The store of cannon on the neighbouring gun-wharf, had an innocent toy-like
appearance, and the one red-coated sentry on
duty over them was a mere toy figure, with a
clock-work movement. As the hot sunlight
sparkled on him he might have passed for the
identical little man who had the little gun, and
whose bullets they were made of lead, lead, lead.

CHAPTER IX

CANTERBURY

" It would be rash not to come on and see the Cathedral."
(Mr. Micawber in *David Copperfield*)

I

CANTERBURY is endeared to us through its association with Agnes Wickfield ; and *David Copperfield*
is the only book in which the ecclesiastical capital
of the county is referred to at any length.

Dickens must have been familiar with it, as he
would probably have visited it from Broadstairs,
where he spent his summer holidays for many
years. But, strange to say, there is no record that
Dickens actually did visit the city prior to writing
David Copperfield in 1849.

In 1850 we find him writing from Broadstairs to
Forster :

> There are Canterbury and all varieties of
> what Leigh Hunt calls " Greenery " within a
> few minutes railroad ride ;

and in the following year, to Charles Knight, in
somewhat the same strain, also from Broadstairs.

> We will make expeditions to Herne Bay,
> Canterbury, where not ? . . . You'll never see
> the country so pretty. . . . Say you'll come.

On 4th November, 1861, he gave a reading there,
and wrote to his daughter Mamie the same evening,
calling it " Windy night " from the Fountain Hotel.

A word of report before I go to bed. An excellent house to-night, and an audience positively perfect. The greatest part of it stalls and an intelligent and delightful response in them, like the touch of a beautiful instrument. "Copperfield" wound up in a real burst of feeling and delight.

A few days later he paid a further compliment to the people of Canterbury in a letter to his sister-in-law, Miss Hogarth.

The most delicate audience I have seen in any provincial place is Canterbury.

With the exception of a reference in *Barnaby Rudge*, when Mr. Varden is endeavouring to get Sim Tappertit out of London on account of his connection with the rioters, and proposes :

If I call him by five o'clock . . . he may get to the Tower Stairs and away by the Gravesend tide-boat before any search is made for him. From there he can easily get on to Canterbury, where your cousin will give him work till this storm has blown over,

and a reference to the Canterbury Pilgrims in Chapter III of *Our Mutual Friend*, and a reference to Mr. Dorrit's grand progress to the coast in the days of his riches, when he was "waylaid at Dartford, pillaged at Gravesend, rifled at Rochester, fleeced at Sittingbourne and sacked at Canterbury," Canterbury's sole claim to Dickensian interest rests with *David Copperfield*.

We have already seen how little David left London on his long walk to his aunt's at Dover ; how he passed through Rochester and Chatham, and we read further that he passed through

the sunny street of Canterbury, dozing as it were in the hot light . . . with . . . its old

houses and gateways, and the stately, grey
Cathedral, with the rooks sailing round the
towers.

When at length he reached his aunt's and it was
thought advisable to send him to school, his aunt
said, " Should you like to go to school at Canterbury ? " and David replied that he would like it
very much, as Canterbury was so near her. So
accordingly to Canterbury he went to the house of
Mr. Wickfield, his aunt's lawyer, the original of
which is said to be at No. 71 St. Dunstan's Street,
near to the West Gate. It is described as
follows :

At length we stopped before a very old house
bulging out over the road ; a house with long
low lattice-windows bulging out still farther,
and beams with carved heads on the ends
bulging out too, so that I fancied the whole
house was leaning forward, trying to see who was
passing on the narrow pavement below. It
was quite spotless in its cleanliness. The old-
fashioned brass knocker on the low arched door,
ornamented with carved garlands of fruit and
flowers, twinkled like a star ; the two stone
steps descending to the door were as white as if
they had been covered with fair linen ; and
all the angles and corners, and carvings and
mouldings, and quaint little panes of glass, and
quainter little windows, though as old as the
hills, were as pure as any snow that ever fell
upon the hills. . . .

In the course of the evening I had rambled
down to the door, and a little way across the
street, that I might have another peep at the
old houses, and the grey Cathedral ; and might
think of my coming through that old city in

my journey, and of my passing the very house I lived in, without knowing it.

At a later date, David tells us :

Coming into Canterbury, I loitered through the old streets with a sober pleasure that calmed my spirits and eased my heart. There were the old signs, the old names over the shops, the old people serving in them. It appeared so long since I had been a schoolboy there, that I wondered the place was so little changed, until I reflected how little I was changed myself.

On what was probably his last visit to Canterbury David writes in Chapter LII :

Early in the morning, I sauntered through the dear old tranquil streets, and again mingled with the shadows of the venerable gateways and churches. The rooks were sailing about the cathedral towers ; and the towers themselves, overlooking many a long unaltered mile of the rich country and its pleasant streams, were cutting the bright morning air, as if there were no such thing as change on earth. Yet the bells, when they sounded, told me sorrowfully of change in everything ; . . . while the reverberations of the bells had hummed through the rusty armour of the Black Prince hanging up within, and, motes upon the deep of Time, had lost themselves in air, as circles do in water.

I looked at the old house from the corner of the street. . . . The early sun was striking edgewise on its gables and lattice-windows, touching them with gold ; and some beams of its old peace seemed to touch my heart.

Of Mr. Micawber's advent at Canterbury we read in Chapter XXXVI :

I am about to establish myself in one of the

provincial towns of our favoured island (where
the society may be described as a happy ad-
mixture of the agricultural and the clerical)
in immediate connection with one of the learned
professions. Mrs. Micawber and our offspring
will accompany me. . . .

" It may be a sacrifice," said Mrs. Micawber,
" to immure one's self in a Cathedral town." . . .

" Oh ! You are going to a Cathedral town ? "
said I.

Mr. Micawber, who had been helping us all,
out of the wash-hand-stand jug, replied :

" To Canterbury. In fact, my dear Copperfield, I have entered into arrangements, by
virtue of which I stand pledged and contracted
to our friend Heep, to assist and serve him in
the capacity of—and to be—his confidential
clerk." . . .

" On Monday next, on the arrival of the four
o'clock afternoon coach at Canterbury, my foot
will be on my native heath—my name,
Micawber ! "

II

Dr. Strong's School, to which David was sent by
his aunt, is said to have had its prototype in the
King's School.

A grave building in a courtyard with a learned
air about it that seemed very well suited to the
stray rooks and jackdaws who came down from
the Cathedral Towers to walk with a clerkly
bearing on the grass plot. . . . Doctor Strong
looked almost as rusty, to my thinking, as the
tall iron rails and gates outside the house : and
almost as stiff and heavy as the great stone

urns that flanked them, and were set up, on
the top of the red brick wall, at regular distances
all round the court, like substantial skittles for
Time to play at. . . .

The school-room was a pretty large hall, on
the quietest side of the house, confronted by
the stately stare of some half-dozen of the great
urns, and commanding a peep of an old secluded
garden belonging to the Doctor, where the
peaches were ripening on the sunny south wall.

What stood for Dr. Strong's house is at No. 1
Lady Wootton's Green.

Uriah Heep's house is said to have been situated
in North Lane—now demolished.

" Here is my humble dwelling, Mr. Copperfield ! "

We entered a low, old-fashioned room, walked
straight into from the street.

Of the Cathedral itself David Copperfield writes :

A moment, and I occupy my place in the
Cathedral, where we all went together, every
Sunday morning, assembling first at School for
that purpose.   The earthy smell, the sunless air,
the sensation of the world being shut out, the
resounding of the organ through the black and
white arched galleries and aisles. . . .

The venerable Cathedral towers, and the old
jackdaws and rooks whose airy voices made
them more retired than perfect silence would
have done ; the battered gateways, once stuck
full of statues, long thrown down and crumbled
away, like the reverential pilgrims who had
gazed upon them : the still rooks, where the
ivied growth of centuries crept over gabled ends
and ruined walls : the ancient houses, the
pastoral landscape of field, orchard and garden ;

everywhere, on everything—I felt the same serene air, the same calm, thoughtful, softening spirit.

Mrs. Micawber, in one of her bursts of confidence to David, informs him :

We saw, I think, the greater part of the Medway. . . . Being so near here, Mr. Micawber was of the opinion that it would be rash not to come on and see the Cathedral. Firstly, on account of its being so well worth seeing, and our never having seen it : and secondly, on account of the great probability of something turning up in a Cathedral city.

The " County Inn " at which Mr. Dick put up was no doubt the Fountain Hotel, at which Dickens stayed on his reading tour in 1861.

Another Canterbury inn, also figuring in *David Copperfield*, where it is described as a " little inn," was no doubt the Sun Inn, close to the Cathedral.

I saw Mr. Dick every alternate Wednesday, when he arrived by Stage Coach at noon, to stay until next morning. . . . Mr. Dick was very partial to Gingerbread. To render his visits more agreeable, my aunt had instructed me to open a credit for him at a cake shop, which was hampered with the stipulation that he should not be served with more than one shilling's worth in the course of any one day. This, and the reference to all his little bills at the county inn where he slept, to my Aunt, before they were paid, induced me to suspect that he was only allowed to rattle his money, and not to spend it.

The quaint little Sun Inn has been identified as the hostelry where Mr. Micawber stayed.

It was a little inn where Mr. Micawber put

up, and he occupied a little room in it, partitioned
off from the commercial room, and strongly
flavoured with tobacco smoke.   I think it was
over the kitchen, because a warm, greasy smell
appeared to come up through the chinks in the
floor, and there was a flabby perspiration on
the walls.   I know it was near the bar, on
account of the smell of spirits and jingling of
glasses.

It was here also that David, his aunt, Mr. Dick,
and Traddles stopped when they went down to
Canterbury to assist Mr. Micawber in the unmasking
of Uriah Heep.   The preliminary appointment with
Mr. Micawber, was, to use his own words,

at the house of public entertainment at Canterbury, where Mrs. Micawber and myself had once
the honour of uniting our voices to yours, in the
well-known strain of the Immortal exciseman
nurtured beyond the Tweed.

And the party journeyed " down to Canterbury by
the Dover Mail."

At the hotel where Mr. Micawber had requested
us to await him, which we got into with some
trouble in the middle of the night, I found a
letter, importing that he would appear in the
morning punctually at half-past nine.   After
which we went shivering, at that uncomfortable
hour, to our respective beds, through various
close passages which smelt as if they had been
steeped for ages in a solution of soup and
stables.

In a later chapter, after Mr. Micawber's triumph,
David writes :

Shall I ever recall that street of Canterbury
on a market day, without recalling him, as he
walked back with us ; expressing, in the hardy

roving manner he assumed, the unsettled habits
of a temporary sojourner in the land ; and
looking at the bullocks, as they came by, with
the eye of an Australian farmer !
The road leading from Canterbury to Ramsgate,
also has an interest.

I had not walked out far enough to be quite
clear of the town, upon the Ramsgate Road,
where there was a good path,
David tells us ; and here it was that he was nailed
by Uriah and the quarrel over Agnes ensued.

At the Church of St. Alphege, in the High Street,
Dr. Strong was married to Annie, a fact that Mrs.
Markleham announced in Chapter XLV.

III

Dolby, in his interesting book, *Charles Dickens
as I Knew Him*, describes a visit to Canterbury
paid by Dickens and a party of friends from Gad's
Hill, and it serves to show the intimacy Dickens had
with the city, and the thoroughness with which he
entertained his friends :

" We drove into Canterbury in the early afternoon, just as the bells of the Cathedral were ringing
for afternoon service. Entering the quiet city
under the old gate at the end of the High Street, it
seemed as though its inhabitants were indulging in
an afternoon's nap after a midday dinner. But
our entry and the clatter of our horses' hoofs roused
them as it had done the people of Rochester, and
they came running to their windows and out into
the streets to learn what so much noise might mean.

" We turned into the bye-street in which the
Fountain Hotel is situated, where the carriages and
horses were to be put up while we explored the city.

" We went first to the Cathedral, where service was just commencing. There was a very small congregation, and we were all disappointed at the careless, half-hearted manner in which the service was performed. The seeming indifference of the officiating clergy jarred most acutely on Dickens's feelings, for he, who did all things so thoroughly, could not conceive how (as he afterwards said) any persons accepting an office, or a trust so important as the proper rendering of our beautiful Cathedral Service, could go through their duties in this mechanical and slip-shod fashion. He returned to this subject on several subsequent occasions. As the service had tended rather to depress than to elevate our spirits, we were all glad to get out into the fresh air of the cloisters, on its termination.

" Being in Canterbury Cathedral, Mr. Dickens considered it necessary to show his friends the many objects of interest to be found there ; and after he had politely but speedily got rid of a tedious verger who wanted to lead the way, he played the part of cicerone himself, in the most genial and learned style in the world.

" Under his pleasant and instructive guidance, the afternoon passed only too quickly, and we stayed so long in the grand old Cathedral that we had but little time to spare for a ramble through the sleepy streets. Some of the Americans were rather disappointed at this, for, knowing the accuracy of Dickens's descriptions, they had shown an extreme curiosity to see and examine for themselves the very house where David Copperfield went to school.

" There are, however, many houses in Canterbury which would answer to Dickens's description of ' Doctor Strong's ' ; and in reply to one of the party who had asked him to point out the particular house, he said, laughingly, that ' there were several that would do.' We took tea at the hotel, and then at about six o'clock started on our homeward journey, Canterbury having by this time quite got over the effects of its day-sleep. The people were enjoying their stroll in the cool of the evening, and the streets presented a much more animated appearance than they had done on our arrival. In the interval between drowsiness and wakefulness, Canterbury had evidently summoned sufficient energy to make inquiries about our party ; and learning that no less a person than Charles Dickens was responsible for having disturbed their slumbers earlier in the day, the good people at once forgave us all, and were quite hearty in their salutations as we left the town."

CHAPTER X

STAPLEHURST AND PADDOCK WOOD

" A Terribly Destructive Accident."
(Postscript to *Our Mutual Friend*)

I

THOSE who read Prefaces—and Dickens's Prefaces throw many interesting side-lights on the author and his work—will remember the allusion to a railway accident in which Mr. and Mrs. Boffin "in their manuscript dress" came near to meeting dire calamity. In *Our Mutual Friend* there is no Preface, but a " Postscript in lieu of a Preface," and the portion referred to is as follows :

On Friday the ninth of June in the present year Mr. and Mrs. Boffin (in their manuscript dress of receiving Mr. and Mrs. Lammle at breakfast) were on the South-Eastern Railway with me, in a terribly destructive accident. When I had done what I could to help others, I climbed back into my carriage—nearly turned over a viaduct, and caught aslant upon the turn—to extricate the worthy couple. They were much soiled, but otherwise unhurt. The same happy result attended Miss Bella Wilfer on her wedding-day, and Mr. Riderhood inspecting Bradley Headstone's red neckerchief as he lay asleep. I remember with devout thankfulness that I can never be much nearer parting company with

my readers for ever, than I was then, until there
shall be written against my life the two words
with which I have this day closed this book—
THE END.

For an account of what befell the train in which
Dickens was travelling (he was returning from a
short holiday in France), we cannot do better than
refer to letters written by him at the time. The
fullest was to his o d friend Thomas M tton, dated
13th June, four days after the occurrence. It was
not all in his handwriting as the note accompanying
it shows :

> Many thanks for your kind words of remem-
> brance.   This is not all in my own hand, because
> I am too much shaken to write many notes.
> Not by the beating and dragging of the carriage
> in which I was—it did not go over, but was
> caught on the turn, among the ruins of the
> bridge—but by the work afterwards to get out
> the dying and dead, which was terrible.

Gad's Hill Place, Higham by Rochester, Kent,
Tuesday, Thirteenth June, 1865.

MY DEAR MITTON,

I should have written to you yesterday or
the day before, if I had been quite up to writing.

I was in the only carriage that did not go over
into the stream. It was caught upon the turn
by some of the ruin of the bridge, and hung
suspended and balanced in an apparently
impossible manner. Two ladies were my fellow-
passengers, an old one and a young one. This
is exactly what passed. You may judge from
it the precise length of the suspense : Suddenly
we were off the rail, and beating the ground as
the car of a half-emptied balloon might. The

old lady cried out, " My God ! " and the young one screamed. I caught hold of them both (the old lady sat opposite and the young one on my left), and said : " We can't help ourselves, but we can be quiet and composed. Pray don't cry out." The old lady immediately answered : " Thank you. Rely upon me. Upon my soul I will be quiet." We were then all tilted down together in a corner of the carriage, and stopped. I said to them thereupon : " You may be sure nothing worse can happen. Our danger must be over. Will you remain here without stirring, while I get out of the window ? "   They both answered quite collectedly, " Yes," and I got out without the least notion what had happened. Fortunately I got out with great caution and stood upon the step. Looking down I saw the bridge gone, and nothing below me but the line of rail.   Some people in the two other compart- ments were madly trying to plunge out of window, and had no idea that there was an open swampy field fifteen feet down below them, and nothing else ! The two guards (one with his face cut) were running up and down on the down side of the bridge (which was not torn up) quite wildly.   I called out to them : " Look at me.   Do stop an instant and look at me, and tell me whether you don't know me."   One of them answered : " We know you very well, Mr. Dickens." " Then," I said, " my good fellow, for God's sake give me your key, and send one of those labourers here, and I'll empty this carriage."   We did it quite safely, by means of a plank or two, and when it was done I saw all the rest of the train, except the two baggage vans, down in the stream. I got into the carriage again for my brandy flask, took off my travelling hat for a basin, climbed down the brickwork and filled my hat with water.

Suddenly I came upon a staggering man covered with blood (I think he must have been flung clean out of his carriage), with such a frightful cut across the skull that I couldn't bear to look at him. I poured some water over his face and gave him some to drink, then gave him some brandy, and laid him down on the grass, and he said, "I am gone," and died afterwards. Then I stumbled over a lady lying on her back against a little pollard-tree, with the blood streaming over her face (which was lead colour) in a number of distinct little streams from the head. I asked her if she could swallow a little brandy and she just nodded, and I gave her some and left her for somebody else. The next time I passed her she was dead. Then a man, examined at the inquest yesterday (who evidently had not the least remembrance of what really passed), came running up to me and implored me to help him find his wife, who was afterwards found dead. No imagination can conceive the ruin of the carriages, or the extraordinary weights under which the people were lying, or the complications into which they were twisted up among iron and wood, and mud and water.

I don't want to be examined at the inquest, and I don't want to write about it. I could do no good either way, and I could only seem to speak about myself, which, of course, I would rather not do. I am keeping very quiet here. I have a—I don't know what to call it—constitutional (I suppose) presence of mind, and was

not in the least fluttered at the time.   I instantly
remembered that I had the MS. of a number
with me, and clambered back into the carriage
for it.   But in writing these scanty words of
recollection I feel the shake and am obliged to
stop.

Ever faithfully

To his friend and neighbour, Mrs. Hulkes, who
had sent him a copy of *The Examiner* with an account
of the accident, he wrote :

I return *The Examiner* with many thanks.
The account is true, except that I had brandy.
By an extraordinary chance I had a bottle and
a half with me.   I slung the half-bottle round
my neck, and carried my hat full of water in my
hands.   But I can understand the describer
(whoever he is) making the mistake in perfect
good faith, and supposing that I called for
brandy, when I really called to the others who
were helping : " I have brandy here."   The
Mr. Dickenson mentioned had changed places
with a Frenchman, who did not like the window
down, a few minutes before the accident.   The
Frenchman was killed, and a labourer and I got
Mr. Dickenson out of a most extraordinary
heap of dark ruins, in which he was jammed
upside down.   He was bleeding at the eyes,
ears, nose, and mouth ; but he didn't seem to
know that afterwards, and of course I didn't
tell him.   In a moment of going over the viaduct
the whole of his pockets were shaken empty !
He had no watch, no chain, no money, no
pocket-book, no handkerchief, when we got him
out.   He had been choking a quarter of an hour
when I heard him groaning.   If I had not had
the brandy to give him at the moment, I think

he would have been done for. As it was, I brought him up to London in the carriage with me, and couldn't make him believe he was hurt. He was the first person whom the brandy saved. As I ran back to the carriage for the whole full bottle, I saw the first two people I had helped lying dead. A bit of shade from the hot sun, into which we got the unhurt ladies, soon had as many dead in it as living.

To Forster he wrote a brief note the very day after : the date is Saturday, Tenth of June, 1865.

I was in the terrific Staplehurst accident yesterday, and worked for hours among the dying and dead. I was in the carriage that did not go over, but went off the line, and hung over the bridge in an inexplicable manner. No words can describe the scene. I am away to Gads.

Forster then continues : Though with characteristic energy he resisted the effects upon himself of that terrible ninth of June, they were for some time evident ; and, up to the day of his death on its fatal fifth anniversary, were perhaps never wholly absent. But very few complaints fell from him. " I am curiously weak—weak as if I were recovering from a long illness." " I begin to feel it more in my head. I sleep well and eat well ; but I write half a dozen notes, and turn faint and sick." " I am getting right, though still low in pulse and very nervous. Driving into Rochester yesterday I felt more shaken than I have since the accident." " I cannot bear railway travelling yet. A perfect conviction against the senses, that the carriage is down on one side (and generally that is the left, and *not* the side on which the carriage in the accident really went over), comes upon me with anything like speed, and is inexpressibly distressing."

To show the effect it had on him three years later, we quote a portion of a letter to Monsieur Cerjat dated 26th August, 1868 :

My escape in the Staplehurst accident of three years ago is not to be obliterated from my nervous system. To this hour I have sudden vague rushes of terror, even when riding in a hansom cab, which are perfectly unreasonable but quite insurmountable. I used to make nothing of driving a pair of horses habitually through the most crowded parts of London. I cannot now drive, with comfort to myself, on the country roads here ; and I doubt if I could ride at all in the saddle. My reading secretary and companion knows so well when one of these odd momentary seizures comes upon me in a railway carriage, that he instantly produces a dram of brandy, which rallies the blood to the heart and generally prevails. I forget whether I ever told you that my watch (a chronometer) has never gone exactly since the accident ?

Dickens's escape was certainly miraculous ; the train had run into a gap made during the repairing of the line, and no less than eight coaches fell into the bed of the river, and were reduced to a mass of shattered woodwork. Ten passengers were either killed outright or drowned, and many were very severely injured.

II

Some years prior to the Staplehurst catastrophe he had introduced a railway tragedy into one of his books, *Dombey and Son* ; and it was doubtless on the South-Eastern Railway that he located it. Carker's wild flight from Dijon, when he had been spurned by Edith, resulted in his crossing to England, in vague fear of pursuit by Mr. Dombey.

The late Rev. Canon Benham in *Memorials of Old Kent* (1907) states :

" Carker's terrible death unmistakedly occurs at Paddock Wood Station. The villain came there intending to get on to the new branch to Maidstone. The place is much built upon now, but as I first remember it there was the inn in which he tarried, just as described, as are some particular features of the station."

He had thought of going down into a remote Country-place he knew, and lying quiet there, while he secretly informed himself of what transpired, and determined how to act. He remembered a certain station on the railway, where he would have to branch off to his place of destination, and where there was a quiet Inn. Here, he indistinctly resolved to tarry and rest.

With this purpose he was soon borne far away from the sea, and deep into the inland green. Arrived at his destination he looked out, and surveyed it carefully. He was not mistaken in his impression of the place. It was a retired spot, on the borders of a little wood. Only one house, newly-built or altered for the purpose, stood there, surrounded by its neat garden ; the small town that was nearest, was some miles away. Here he alighted then ; and going straight into the tavern, unobserved by any one, secured two rooms up stairs communicating with each other, and sufficiently retired.

From his window he could hear and see the railway, which had an irresistible attraction for him ; he was unable to rest, so he went out and " lounged on the brink of it, marking the way the

12

train had gone, by the yet smoking cinders that were lying in its track."

After a lounge of some half hour in the direction by which it had disappeared, he turned and walked the other way—still keeping to the brink of the road—past the inn garden, and a long way down; looking curiously at the bridges, signals, lamps, and wondering when another Devil would come by.

A trembling of the ground, and quick vibration in his ears; a distant shriek; a dull light advancing, quickly changed to two red eyes, and a fierce fire, dropping glowing coals; an irresistible bearing on of a great roaring and dilating mass; a high wind, and a rattle—another come and gone, and he holding to a gate, as if to save himself!

He waited for another, and for another. He walked back to his former point, and back again to that, and still, through the wearisome vision of his journey, looked for these approaching monsters. He loitered about the station, waiting until one should stay to call there; and when one did, and was detached for water, he stood parallel with it, watching its heavy wheels and brazen front, and thinking what a cruel power and might it had. Ugh! To see the great wheels slowly turning, and to think of being run down and crushed!

He returned to the inn, and spent a restless night, waiting for the early morning to come, and with it the train for his destination.

He paid the money for his journey to the country-place he had thought of; and was walking to and fro, alone, looking along the lines of iron, across the valley in one direction, and

towards a dark bridge near at hand in the other ;
when, turning in his walk, where it was bounded
by one end of the wooden stage on which he
paced up and down, he saw the man from whom
he had fled, emerging from the door by which
he himself had entered there. And their eyes met.

In the quick unsteadiness of the surprise, he
staggered, and slipped on to the road below him.
But recovering his feet immediately, he stepped
back a pace or two upon that road, to interpose
some wider space between them, and looked at
his pursuer, breathing short and quick.

He heard a shout—another—saw the face
change from its vindictive passion to a faint
sickness and terror—felt the earth tremble—
knew in a moment that the rush was come—
uttered a shriek—looked round—saw the red
eyes, bleared and dim, in the daylight, close upon
him—was beaten down, caught up, and whirled
away upon a jagged mill, that spun him round
and round, and struck him limb from limb, and
licked his stream of life up with its fiery heat,
and cast his mutilated fragments in the air.

Paddock Wood Station may certainly have been
in Dickens's mind when writing this chapter. He
was well acquainted with it, as we find him writing
to Forster from Broadstairs on one occasion in 1848 :

You will come down booked for Maidstone
(I will meet you at Paddock Wood), and we will
go thither in company over a most beautiful
little line of railroad. The eight miles' walk
from Maidstone to Rochester, and a visit to the
Druidical altar on the wayside, are charming.
This could be accomplished on the Tuesday ; and
Wednesday we might look about us at Chatham,
coming home by Cobham on Thursday. . . .

CHAPTER XI

BROADSTAIRS

" Our English Watering Place."
(Reprinted Pieces)

I

It was in the autumn of 1837 that Dickens and his
wife went for their first seaside holiday to Broadstairs, which was then quite a retired spot and
nothing approaching the importance it has since
achieved. They stayed at No. 12 (now No. 31)
High Street, and the following is an extract from a
letter to Forster dated September the third :

I am much better, and hope to begin Pickwick No. 18 to-morrow. You will imagine how
queer I must have been when I tell you that I
have been compelled for four-and-twenty mortal
hours to abstain from porter or other malt
liquor ! ! I done it though—really. . . . I
have discovered that the landlord of The Albion
has delicious hollands (but what is that to *you* for
you cannot sympathise with my feelings), and
that a cobbler who lives opposite to my bedroom window is a Roman Catholic, and gives
an hour and a half to his devotions every morning behind his counter. I have walked upon
the sands at low-water from this place to
Ramsgate, and sat upon the same at high ditto
till I have been flayed with the cold. I have
seen ladies and gentlemen walking upon the

earth in slippers of buff, and pickling themselves in the sea in complete suits of the same. I have seen stout gentlemen looking at nothing through powerful telescopes for hours, and when at last they saw a cloud of smoke, fancying a steamer behind it, and going home comfortable and happy. I have found out that our next neighbour has a wife and something else under the same roof with the rest of his furniture—the wife deaf and blind, and the something else given to drinking. And if you ever get to the end of this letter *you* will find out that I subscribe myself on paper as on everything else (some atonement perhaps for its length and absurdity), etc.

No doubt Forster visited him at that time, for we find a reference to it in a letter of 9th September, 1839, in which Dickens reminds him of the " Albion Hotel where we had that merry night two years ago."

The August and September of the year following were also spent at Broadstairs—probably also at High Street ; he was busy on *Nicholas Nickleby* and *Oliver Twist* at the time. The house in High Street has the following tablet upon it :

Charles Dickens
lived here
And wrote part of " The Pickwick Papers "
1837

The Albion Hotel is also in the High Street ; it bears the following tablet :

Charles Dickens
stayed here
1839, 1840, 1842, 1843, 1845, 1849, 1859,
and wrote part of " Nicholas Nickleby "

When Dickens visited Broadstairs in 1839, 1840,

1842, and 1843, he stayed at No. 40 Albion Street, two doors from what was then the Albion Hotel, or " Ballards," as it was called. This house was subsequently incorporated in the hotel, as Dickens explains to his daughters in his letter of 1859 quoted on page 197.

The first work done at Albion Street was the completion of *Nicholas Nickleby*, for, to quote Forster, " The close of the story was written at Broadstairs, from which (he had taken a house ' two doors from the Albion-hotel, where we had that merry night, two years ago ') he wrote to me on the 9th September, 1839 " :

> I am hard at it, but these windings-up wind slowly, and I shall think I have done great things if I have entirely finished by the 20th. Chapman and Hall came down yesterday with Browne's sketches, and dined here. They imparted their intentions as to a Nicklebeian fête which will make you laugh heartily—so I reserve them till you come. It has been blowing great guns for the last three days, and last night (I wish you could have seen it !) there was such a sea ! I staggered down to the pier, and, creeping under the lee of a large boat which was high and dry, watched it breaking for nearly an hour. Of course I came back wet through.

June of the next year found him at Broadstairs once more, and Forster quotes a portion of a letter which he says gives " characteristic expression of his invariable habit upon entering any new abode, whether to stay in it for days or for years " :

> Before I tasted bit or drop yesterday, I set out my writing table with extreme taste and neatness, and improved the disposition of the furniture generally.

Forster tells us he stayed in the town until the end of June when Maclise the artist and himself " joined him for the pleasure of posting back home by way of his favourite Chatham, Rochester and Cobham, where we passed two agreeable days in revisiting well-remembered scenes."

To Maclise, Dickens had written from Broadstairs on 2nd June, 1840 :

> My foot is in the house,
> My bath is on the sea,
> And, before I take a souse,
> Here's a single note to thee.

It merely says that the sea is in a state of extraordinary sublimity ; that this place is, as the Guide Book most justly observes, " unsurpassed for the salubrity of the refreshing breezes, which are wafted on the ocean's pinions from far-distant shores." That we are all right after the perils and voyages of yesterday. That the sea is rolling away in front of the window at which I indite this epistle, and that everything is as fresh and glorious as fine weather and a splendid coast can make it. Bear these recommendations in mind, and shunning Talfourdian pledges, come to the bower which is shaded for you in the one-pair front, where no chair or table has four legs of the same length, and where no drawers will open till you have pulled the pegs off, and then they keep open and won't shut again. Come ! I can no more.

He was again at Broadstairs in August of the same year, when Forster tells us, that failing to get Fort House, he rented Lawn House. It is therefore probable that in the June he was still at Albion Street. The following extract is from Forster's *Life of Dickens* :

" At the opening of September he was again at the little watering-place. The residence he most desired there, Fort House, stood prominently at the top of a breezy hill on the road to Kingsgate, with a corn-field between it and the sea, and this in many subsequent years he always occupied ; but he was fain to be content as yet with Lawn House, a smaller villa between the hill and the corn-field from which he now wrote of his attentions to Mr. Sampson Brass's sister. ' I have been at work of course ' (2nd September) ' and have just finished a number. I have effected a reform by virtue of which we breakfast at a quarter before eight, so that I get to work at half-past, and am commonly free by one o'clock or so, which is a great happiness.' "

Lawn House is marked with the following tablet :

Here
Charles Dickens
lived and wrote
Part of " Barnaby Rudge," 1841

This is hardly ample enough, as Dickens stayed in Lawn House also in 1840 and wrote part of *The Old Curiosity Shop* there. The year 1841 again saw him at Broadstairs, from August until October, when he decided to visit America in the January following. In the August he wrote a characteristically descriptive letter to Forster, as follows :

It is the brightest day you ever saw. The sun is sparkling on the water so that I can hardly bear to look at it. The tide is in, and the fishing-boats are dancing like mad. Upon the green-topped cliffs the corn is cut and piled in shocks ; and thousands of butterflies are fluttering about, taking the bright little red flags at the mastheads for flowers, and panting with delight accordingly. (Here the Inimitable, unable to resist the brilliancy out of doors, breaketh off, rusheth to the machines, and plungeth into the sea. Returning, he proceedeth.)

II

On returning from America in 1842 and finding his London House still in the possession of Sir John Wilson, to whom he had let it during his absence, he went for a short time to Broadstairs, staying at the Albion Street address. Here he was busy with *American Notes*, and from here he wrote to Forster on the 7th August :

I have been reading Tennyson all this morning on the seashore. Among other trifling effects, the waters have dried up as they did of old, and shown me all the mermen and mermaids, at the bottom of the ocean ; together with millions of queer creatures, half-fish and half-fungus, looking down into all manner of coral caves and seaweed conservatories ; and staring in with their great dull eyes at every open nook and loophole. Who else, too, could conjure up such a close to the extraordinary and as Landor would say ' most woonderful ' series of pictures in the ' dream of fair women ' as—

Squadrons and squares of men in brazen plates,
Scaffolds, still sheets of water, divers woes,
Ranges of glimmering vaults with iron gates,
And hushed seraglios !

I am getting on pretty well, but it was so glittering and sunshiny yesterday, that I was forced to make holiday.
In September he came back to London   The sea

was so rough that he had no choice but to return by land. " No steamer can come out of Ramsgate and the Margate boat lay all night with all her passengers on board," he wrote at the time. " I have determined to leave here to-morrow . . . and have engaged an omnibus to bring the whole caravan by the overland route."

The following year found him again true to Broadstairs, an amusing description of which he gave to his American friend, Professor Felton, as follows :

This is a little fishing-place ; intensely quiet ; built on a cliff, whereon—in the centre of a tiny semicircular bay—our house stands ; the sea rolling and dashing under the windows. Seven miles out are the Goodwin Sands (you've heard of the Goodwin Sands ?) whence floating lights perpetually wink after dark, as if they were carrying on intrigues with the servants. Also there is a big lighthouse called the North Foreland on a hill behind the village, a severe parsonic light, which reproves the young and giddy floaters, and stares grimly out upon the sea. Under the cliff are rare good sands, where all the children assemble every morning and throw up impossible fortifications, which the sea throws down again at high water. Old gentlemen and ancient ladies flirt after their own manner in two reading-rooms and on a great many scattered seats in the open air. Other old gentlemen look all day through telescopes and never see anything. In a bay-window in a one-pair sits, from nine o'clock to one, a gentleman with rather long hair and no neckcloth, who writes and grins as if he thought he were very funny indeed. His name is Boz. At one he disappears, and presently emerges from a bathing machine, and may be seen—a kind of salmon-coloured porpoise—splashing about in the ocean. After that he may be seen in another bay-window on the ground-floor, eating a strong lunch ; after that, walking a dozen miles or so, or lying on his back in the sand reading a book. Nobody bothers him unless they know he is disposed to be talked to ; and I am told he is very comfortable indeed. He's as brown as a berry, and they *do* say is a small fortune to the innkeeper who sells beer and cold punch. But this is mere rumour. Sometimes he goes up to London (eighty miles, or so, away), and then I'm told there is a sound in Lincoln's Inn Fields at night, as of men laughing, together with a clinking of knives and forks and wine-glasses.

His next visit was two years later (1845), and two years later still he spent June to October there, living in Chandos Place ; of the exact house, we are not certain, it was probably No. 1 or No. 6.

To Miss Power he wrote at that time (July 2nd) :

I am looking out upon a dark gray sea, with a keen north-east wind blowing it in shore. It is more like late autumn than midsummer, and there is a howling in the air as if the latter were in a very hopeless state indeed. The very Banshee of Midsummer is rattling the windows drearily while I write. There are no visitors in the place but children, and they (my own included) have all got the hooping-cough, and go about the beach choking incessantly. A miserable wanderer lectured in a library last night about astronomy ; but being in utter solitude he snuffed out the transparent planets he had brought with him in a box and fled in disgust. A white mouse and a little tinkling box of music that stops at " come " in the melody of the Buffalo Gals, and can't play " out to-night " are the only amusements left.

.   .   .   .   .   .

Some wild beasts (in cages) have come down here, and involved us in a whirl of dissipation. A young lady in complete armour—at least, in something that shines very much, and is exceedingly scaley—goes into the den of ferocious lions, tigers, leopards, etc., and pretends to go to sleep upon the principal lion, upon which a rustic keeper, who speaks through his nose, exclaims, " Behold the abazid power of woobad ! " and we all applaud tumultuously.

On the 5th September we find a letter to Forster, as follows :

A sea fog here which prevents one's seeing the low water mark. A circus on the cliffs to the right, and of course I have a box to-night. . . . A shipwreck on the Goodwin Sands last Sunday.

III

It was during this visit (1847) that he first began to complain of the great noise in the streets, which rendered writing rather difficult. To Forster he wrote :

Vagrant music is getting to that height here, and is so impossible to be escaped from, that I fear Broadstairs and I must part company in time to come. Unless it pours of rain, I cannot write half-an-hour without the most excruciating organs, fiddles, bells, or glee-singers. There is a violin of the most torturing kind under the window now (time, ten in the morning) and an Italian box of music on the steps—both in full blast.

However, in spite of this, the charm of Broadstairs still continued to hold him. The next year he spent an idle summer there, with only *The Haunted Man* to finish.

In the August there was the carriage accident near Margate (see page 207), but fortunately this was not serious, and he had a succession of good friends visiting him, including Leech, Mark Lemon, and Forster, to keep him merry. We are reasonably jolly," he wrote, " but rurally so ; going to bed o' nights at ten and bathing o' mornings at half past seven."

In 1849 he was in the throes of *David Copperfield*, first at Brighton, and then at Broadstairs again. This was in the July of that year. As soon as he was in Broadstairs, he became more settled in his mind about the book and decided to put a great part of the MS. of his own life, on which he had been busy some time previously, into Number 4 of the story ; this was Chapter XI, which is mostly autobiographical.

In the July of that year Dickens sought a change from Broadstairs, and visited the Isle of Wight for the summer ; but he found the air too relaxing ; his daughter Mamie was taken ill, so in the September the family returned to Broadstairs, with what result the following letter shows :

Such a night and day of rain I should think the oldest inhabitant never saw ! and yet, in the ould formiliar Broadstairs, I somehow or other don't mind it much. The change has done Mamey a world of good, and I have begun to sleep again. As for news, you might as well ask me for Dolphins. Nobody in Broadstairs—to speak of. Certainly nobody in Ballard's. We are in the part, which is the house next door to the hotel itself, that we once had for three years running, and just as quiet and snug now as it was then.

The location of Betsey Trotwood at Dover was purely imaginary, as the original was Mary Strong, who lived in the house in Nuckall's Place, Broadstairs, now called Dickens House and marked with a tablet inscribed as follows :

In this house lived
the original of
Betsey Trotwood in David Copperfield
by Charles Dickens
1849

The gardens now in front of the house, which faces the sea, were meadow-land in those days, and Miss Strong, it is said, had as decided an antipathy to donkeys as Miss Betsey.

In July, 1850, Dickens was at last able to secure Fort House from the July for a few months, and here *David Copperfield* was completed.

The house has undergone several alterations since then, including the altogether unnecessary change of name to Bleak House—a tribute to Dickens, no doubt ; but it was not the Bleak House of the story, nor was any portion of *Bleak House* planned or written there.

On an outer wall of the house is a granite tablet bearing a bronze bust of Dickens, encircled by a wreath bound with ribbons upon which are inscribed the names of some of the works. It is a pity that *Barnaby Rudge* and *The Old Curiosity Shop*, both partly written at Broadstairs, should be omitted and *Bleak House* and other works having no association with the place included.

The following letter was written to Mrs. Dickens in September, 1850, from Fort House :

Yesterday Charles Knight, White, Forster, Charley and I walked to Richborough Castle and back. Knight dined with us afterwards ; and the Whites, the Bicknells, and Mrs. Gibson came in in the evening and played vingt-et-un.

Having no news I must tell you a story of Sydney. The children, Georgy, and I were out in the garden on Sunday evening (by-the-bye, I made a beautiful passage down, and got to Margate a few minutes after one), when I asked Sydney if he would go to the railroad and see if Forster was coming. As he answered very boldly " yes," I opened the garden-gate, upon which he set off alone as fast as his legs would carry him ; and being pursued, was not over-taken until he was through the Lawn House Archway, when he was still going on at full speed—I can't conceive where. Being brought back in triumph, he made a number of fictitious starts, for the sake of being overtaken again, and we made a regular game of it. At last, when he and Ally had run away, instead of running after them, we came into the garden, shut the gate and crouched down on the ground. Presently we heard them come back and say to each other with some alarm, " Why, the gate's shut, and they're all gone ! " Ally began in a dismayed way to cry out, but the phenomenon shouting, " Open the gate ! " sent an enormous stone flying into the garden (among our heads) by way of alarming the establishment. I thought it a wonderful piece

of character, showing great readiness of resource·
He would have fired a perfect battery of stones,
or very likely have broken the pantry window,
I think, if we hadn't let him in.

The early summer of 1851 saw him again at Fort
House, where he stayed until the October. An
early letter (1st June) to Forster said :

It is more delightful here than I can express.
Corn growing, larks singing, garden full of
flowers, fresh air on the sea.—O it is wonderful !
Why can't you come down next Saturday
(bringing work) and go back with me on
Wednesday for the Copperfield banquet ?

This was his last regular visit to Broadstairs ;
the growth of the place, and " the plague of itinerant
music," as Forster puts it, made it impossible for
him to find there the seclusion he sought for his
more important work.

To Lord Carlisle, who visited him there in July,
he wrote the following description of Broadstairs
and instructions for getting there :

The general character of Broadstairs as to
size and accommodation was happily expressed
by Miss Eden, when she wrote to the Duke of
Devonshire (as he told me), saying how grateful
she felt to a certain sailor, who asked leave to
see her garden, for not plucking it bodily up,
and sticking it in his button-hole.

As we think of putting mignonette-boxes
outside the windows for the younger children
to sleep in by-and-by, I am afraid we should
give your servant the cramp if we hardily undertook to lodge him. But in cases you should
decide to bring one, he is easily disposable
hard by.

Don't come by the boat. It is rather tedious,

and both departs and arrives at inconvenient hours. There is a railway train from the Dover terminus to Ramsgate, at half-past twelve in the day, which will bring you in three hours. Another at half-past four in the afternoon. If you will tell me by which you come (I hope the former) I will await you at the terminus with my little brougham.

You will have for a night-light in the room we shall give you, the North Foreland lighthouse. That and the sea and air are our only lions. It is a very rough little place, but a very pleasant one, and you will make it pleasanter than ever to me.

Other visitors were Charles Knight and Douglas Jerrold ; the following is an extract from a letter to the former :

You say you are coming down to look for a place next week. Now, Jerrold says he is coming on Thursday, by the cheap express at half-past twelve, to return with me for the play early on Monday morning. Can't you make that holiday too ? I have promised him our only spare bed, but we'll find you a bed hard by, and shall be delighted " to eat and drink you," as an American once wrote to me. We will make expeditions to Herne Bay, Canterbury, where not ? and drink deep draughts of fresh air. Come ! They are beginning to cut the corn. You will never see the country so pretty. If you stay in town these days, you'll do nothing. I feel convinced you'll not buy the " Memoirs of a Man of Quality." Say you'll come !

To Frank Stone and Henry Austin he wrote in the September describing a wreck on the Goodwin Sands in the following words :

13

You never saw such a sight as the sands between this and Margate presented yesterday. This day fortnight a steamer laden with cattle going from Rotterdam to the London market, was wrecked on the Goodwins—on which occasion, by the bye, the coming in at night of our Salvage Luggers laden with dead cattle, which were hoisted up upon the pier where they lay in heaps, was a most picturesque and striking sight. The sea since Wednesday has been very rough, blowing in straight upon the land. Yesterday, the shore was strewn with hundreds of oxen, sheep, and pigs (and with bushels upon bushels of apples), in every state and stage of decay—burst open, rent asunder, lying with their stiff hoofs in the air, or with their great ribs yawning like the wrecks of ships—tumbled and beated out of shape, and yet with a horrible sort of humanity about them. Hovering among these carcases was every kind of water-side blunderer, pulling the horns out, getting the hides off, chopping the hoofs with poleaxes, etc., etc., attended by no end of donkey carts, and spectral horses with scraggy necks, galloping wildly up and down as if there were something maddening in the stench. I never beheld such a demoniacal business !

.   .   .   .   .

A great to-do here. A steamer lost on the Goodwins yesterday, and our men bringing in no end of dead cattle and sheep. I stood a supper for them last night, to the unbounded gratification of Broadstairs. They came in from the wreck very wet and tired, and very much disconcerted by the nature of their prize —which, I suppose, after all, will have to be recommitted to the sea, when the hides and tallow are secured. One lean-faced boatman murmured, when they were all ruminative over the bodies as they lay on the pier : " Couldn't sassages be made on it ? " but retired in confusion shortly afterwards, overwhelmed by the execrations of the bystanders.

IV

As we have seen, over a period of fourteen years —with only a year or two's interval, he was faithful to the little Kentish coast town, and he took a fond farewell of it in a paper in *Household Words* for 2nd August, 1851, entitled " Our Watering Place " :

Half awake and half asleep, this idle morning in our sunny window on the edge of a chalk-cliff in the old-fashioned watering-place to which we are a faithful resorter, we feel a lazy inclination to sketch its picture.

The place seems to respond. Sky, sea, beach, and village, lie as still before us as if they were sitting for the picture. It is dead low-water. A ripple plays among the ripening corn upon the cliff, as if it were faintly trying from recollection to imitate the sea ; and the world of butter-flies hovering over the crop of radishseed are as restless in their little way as the gulls are in their larger manner when the wind blows. But the ocean lies winking in the sunlight like a drowsy lion—its glassy waters scarcely curve upon the shore—the fishing-boats in the tiny harbour are all stranded in the mud—our two colliers (our watering-place has a maritime trade employing that amount of shipping) have not

an inch of water within a quarter of a mile of
them, and turn, exhausted, on their sides, like
faint fish of an antediluvian species. Rusty
cables and chains, ropes and rings, undermost
parts of posts and piles and confused timber-
defences against the waves, lie strewn about,
in a brown litter of tangled sea-weed and fallen
cliff which looks as if a family of giants had been
making tea here for ages, and had observed an
untidy custom of throwing their tea-leaves on
the shore.

In truth, our watering-place itself has been
left somewhat high and dry by the tide of years.
Concerned as we are for its honour, we must
reluctantly admit that the time when this pretty
little semi-coloured sweep of houses tapering off
at the end of the wooden pier into a point in the
sea, was a gay place, and when the lighthouse
overlooking it shone at daybreak on company
dispersing from public balls, is but dimly
traditional now.   There is a bleak chamber in
our watering-place which is yet called the
Assembly " Rooms " and understood to be
available on hire for balls or concerts.

.   .   .   .   .

We have a pier—a queer old wooden pier,
fortunately without the slightest pretensions to
architecture, and very picturesque in conse-
quence.   Boats are hauled up upon it, ropes are
coiled all over it ; lobster-pots, nets, masts,
oars, spars, sails, ballast, and rickety capstans,
make a perfect labyrinth of it.

.   .   .   .   .

We have an excellent hotel—capital baths,
warm, cold, and shower—first-rate bathing-

machines—and as good butchers, bakers, and grocers, as heart could desire. They all do business, it is to be presumed, from motives of philanthropy, but it is quite certain that they are all being ruined. Their interest in strangers, and their politeness under ruin, bespeak their amiable nature. You would say so if you only saw the baker helping a new comer to find suitable apartments.

You would hardly guess which is the main street of our watering-place, but you may know it by its being always stopped up with donkey-chaises. Whenever you come here, and see harnessed donkeys eating clover out of barrows drawn completely across a narrow thoroughfare, you may be quite sure you are in our High Street. Our Police you may know by his uniform, likewise by his never on any account interfering with anybody—especially the tramps and vagabonds.

His last visit was some eight years later ; he was far from well at the time, as he wrote to Forster, " I have an instinctive feeling that nothing but the sea will restore me." His friend Wilkie Collins and his brother were at Broadstairs at the time, and to them he wrote, " Nothing but sea air and sea water will set me right. I want to come to Broadstairs next Wednesday by the mid-day train and stay till Monday." Accordingly, Broadstairs welcomed him once again, and again he stayed at the Albion Hotel, from which place he wrote to his two daughters :

Albion, Broadstairs,
Friday, second September, 1859.
MY DEAREST MAMIE & KATIE,
I have been " moved " here, and am now

(Ballard having added to the hotel a house we lived in three years) in our old dining-room and sitting-room, and our old drawing-room as a bedroom. My cold is so bad, both in my throat and in my chest, that I can't bathe in the sea ; Tom Collin dissuaded me—thought it " bad "— but I get a heavy shower-bath at Mrs. Crampton's every morning. The baths are still hers and her husband's, but they have retired and live in " Nickells "—are going to give a stained-glass window, value three hundred pounds, to St. Peter's Church. Tom Collin is of opinion that the Miss Dickenses has growed two fine young women—leastwise, asking pardon, ladies. An evangelical family of most disagreeable girls prowl about here and trip people up with tracts, which they put in the paths with stones upon them to keep them from blowing away. Charles Collins and I having seen a bill yesterday— about a mesmeric young lady who did feats, one of which was set forth in the bill, in a line by itself, as

THE RIGID LEGS

—were overpowered with curiosity, and resolved to go. It came off in the Assembly Room, now more exquisitely desolate than words can describe. Eighteen shillings was the " take." Behind a screen among the company, we heard mysterious gurglings of water before the entertainment began, and then a slippery sound which occasioned me to whisper C. C. (who laughed in the most ridiculous manner) " Soap." It proved to be the young lady washing herself. She must have been wonderfully dirty, for she took a world of trouble, and didn't come out clean after all—in a wretched dirty muslin frock, with blue ribbons. She was the alleged mesmeriser, and a boy who distributed bills the alleged mesmerised. It was a most preposterous imposition, but more ludicrous than any poor sight I ever saw. The boy is clearly out of pantomime, and when he pretended to be in the mesmeric state, made the company back by going in among them head over heels, backwards, half-a-dozen times, in a most insupportable way. The pianist had struck; and the manner in which the lecturer implored " some lady " to play a " polker " and the manner in which no lady would; and in which the few ladies who were there sat with their hats on, and the elastic under their chins, as if it were going to blow, is never to be forgotten. I have been writing all the morning, and am going for a walk to Ramsgate. This is a beast of a letter, but I am not well, and have been addling my head.

Ever, dear Girls,
Your affectionate Father.

CHAPTER XII

OTHER THANET TOWNS

" Now you really must come, seeing only is believing "
(Letter to Forster).

I

THE larger watering-places of Thanet, Ramsgate,
and Margate had little charm for Dickens; he
preferred the quietude offered him by Broadstairs,
the situation of which, midway between the two
towns, enabled him to visit either during an afternoon walk. Thus we find him referring to Ramsgate
during his first visit to Broadstairs in 1837:

> I have walked upon the sands at low-water
> from this place to Ramsgate, and sat upon the
> same at high-ditto till I have been flayed with
> the cold.

But we cannot find he ever paid more than
fleeting visits to the town. In 1845 he wrote to
Forster:

> I went to a circus at Ramsgate on Saturday
> night, where *Mazeppa* was played in three long
> acts without an H in it; as if for a wager.
> Evven, and edds, and orrors, and ands, were as
> plentiful as blackberries; but the letter H was
> neither whispered in Evven, nor muttered in
> Ell, nor permitted to dwell in any form on the
> confines of the sawdust.

There are, however, sundry references to

Ramsgate in the novels—more particularly in the *Sketches by Boz,* and from the knowledge displayed of Ramsgate and Pegwell Bay in " The Tuggses at Ramsgate," published in 1836, it is probable that Dickens had visited the town prior to his stay in Broadstairs in 1837.

This story gives an amusing account of the holiday spent at Ramsgate by the Tuggs family to celebrate their inheritance of twenty thousand pounds. Where shall they go ; Gravesend was low, Margate too full of tradespeople, " Ramsgate ? . . . To be sure ; how stupid they must have been not to have thought of that before ! Ramsgate was just the place of all others."

Two months after this conversation, the City of London Ramsgate steamer was running gaily down the river. Her flag was flying, her band was playing, her passengers were conversing. everything about her seemed gay and lively. No wonder, the Tuggses were on board. . . . A most delightful conversation, aided by these agreeable stimulants, was prolonged until they ran alongside Ramsgate Pier. . . .

The sun was shining brightly—the sea, dancing to its own music, rolled merrily in ; crowds of people promenaded to and fro ; young ladies tittered, old ladies talked, nursemaids displayed their charms to the greatest possible advantage, and their sweet little charges ran up and down, and to and fro and in and out, under the feet and between the legs of the assembled concourse, in the most playful and exhilarating manner possible. There were old gentlemen trying to make out objects through long telescopes, and young ones making objects of themselves in open shirt-collars ; ladies carrying about portable chairs, and portable chairs carrying about invalids. Parties were waiting on the pier for parties who had come by the steam-boat ; and nothing was to be heard but talking, laughing, welcoming, and merriment.

    .   .   .   .   .

If the pier had presented a scene of life and bustle to the Tuggses on their first landing at Ramsgate, it was far surpassed by the appearance of the sands on the morning after their arrival. It was a fine, bright, clear day, with a light breeze from the sea. There were the same ladies and gentlemen, the same children, the same nursemaids, the same telescopes, the same portable chairs ; the ladies were employed in needle-work, or watch-guard making, or knitting, or reading novels : the gentlemen were reading newspapers and magazines, the children were digging holes in the sand with wooden spades, and collecting water therein : the nursemaids, with their youngest charges in arms, were running in after the waves, and then running back with the waves after them : and now and then a little sailing-boat either departed with a gay and talkative cargo of passengers, or returned with a very silent, and particularly uncomfortable-looking one.

    .   .   .   .   .

The library was crowded. There were the same ladies and the same gentlemen that had been on the sands in the morning, and on the pier the day before. There were young ladies in maroon-coloured gowns and black velvet bracelets, dispensing fancy articles in the shop, and presiding over games of chance in the concert - room. There were marriageable daughters and marriage-making mammas, gaming, and promenading, and turning over music, and flirting. There were some male beaux doing the sentimental in whispers, and others doing the ferocious in moustaches.

. . . . .

Thus passed the evening : and thus passed the days and the evenings of the Tuggs's and the Waters's, for six weeks afterwards. Sands in the morning—donkeys at noon : pier in the afternoon—library at night ; and the same people everywhere.

II

Pegwell Bay is, as it always was, a favourite excursion from Ramsgate ; it is under two miles along the coast in a westerly direction.

It was the bogus Captain Waters who proposed the trip to the Tuggses.

" What do you think of doing with yourselves this morning ? " enquired the captain. " Shall we lunch at Pegwell ? "

" I should like that very much indeed," interposed Mrs. Tuggs. She had never heard of Pegwell before ; but the word " lunch " had reached her ears, and it sounded very agreeably.

" How shall we go ? " enquired the captain : " it's too warm to walk."

" A shay ? " suggested Mr. Joseph Tuggs.

" Chaise," whispered Mr. Cymon.

" I should think one would be enough," said Joseph Tuggs aloud, quite unconscious of the meaning of the correction. " However, two shays, if you like."

. . . . .

It was a delightful party to be sure ! Mr. and Mrs. Tuggs, and the captain, had ordered lunch in the little garden behind—small saucers of large shrimps, dabs of butter, crusty loaves, and bottled ale. The sky was without a cloud, there were flower-pots and turf before them ; and the sea at the foot of the cliff, stretching away as far as the eye could discern anything at all, and vessels in the distance with sails as white, and as small, as nicely got-up cambric handkerchiefs. The shrimps were delightful, the ale better, and the captain even more pleasant than either. Mrs. Captain Waters was in *such* spirits after lunch ; chasing, first the captain across the turf, and among the flower-pots, and then Mr. Cymon Tuggs, and then Miss Tuggs, laughing too, quite boisterously. But, as the captain said, it didn't matter : who knew what they were, there ? For all the people of the house knew, they might be common people. To which Mr. Joseph Tuggs responded, " To be be sure," and then they went down the steep wooden steps a little further on, which lead to the bottom of the cliff, and looked at the crabs, and the seaweed and the eels, till it was more than fully time to go back to Ramsgate again.

III

The sister town of Margate comes in for almost an equal amount of mention by Dickens in the *Sketches by Boz*, although no one special story is devoted to it, as was the case with Ramsgate. The reason was, perhaps that it not then achieved the reputation it obtained later on. Mrs. Tuggs simply sneered at Margate when it was suggested

for the family holiday : " Margate ? . . . Worse
and worse—nobody there but tradespeople," she
said.

There are two references to the Margate Theatre
in letters of a characteristic nature written to
Forster and which appear in the *Life of Dickens*.

The first is in 1842, when Dickens wrote to
Forster from Broadstairs :

> The Margate theatre is open every evening,
> and the four Patagonians (see Goldsmith's
> Essays) are performing thrice a week at
> Ranelagh. . . .
> Now you really must come. Seeing only is
> believing, very often isn't that, and even being
> the thing falls a long way short of believing it.
> Mrs. Nickleby herself once asked me, as you
> know, if I really believed there ever was such a
> woman ; but there'll be no more belief, either
> in me or my descriptions, after what I have to
> tell of our excellent friend's tragedy, if you
> don't come and have it played again for yourself
> ' by particular desire.' We saw it last night,
> and oh ! if you had but been with us !

Five years later Forster received another letter,
also from Broadstairs, dated 10th September, 1847,
on which he remarked : " He closed with a mention
of improvements in the Margate theatre since his
memorable last visit. In the past two years it
had been managed by a son of the great comedian,
Dowton, with whose name it is pleasant to connect
this note " :

> We went to the manager's benefit on Wed-
> nesday, *As you like it*, really very well done,
> and a most excellent house. Mr. Dowton
> delivered a sensible and modest kind of speech
> on the occasion setting forth his conviction that

a means of instruction and entertainment
possessing such a literature as the stage of
England, could not pass away ; and that what
inspired great minds, and delighted great men,
two thousand years ago, and did the same in
Shakespeare's day, must have within itself a
principle of life superior to the whim and fashion
of the hour.   And with that, and with cheers,
he retired.   He really seems a most respectable
man, and he has cleared out this dust hole of a
theatre into something like decency.

The journey from London to the Thanet towns
was usually made by water from London Bridge,
and this was the way Dickens most often came ;
and he gives descriptions of the incidents of such
journeys not only in " The Tuggses at Ramsgate,"
already quoted, but in " The River " and " The
Steam Excursion," both in *Sketches by Boz.*

In *Bleak House* reference is made to the popularity
of the Thanet towns for seaside holidays.

It is the hottest long vacation known for many
years.   All the young clerks are madly in love,
and, according to their various degrees, pine for
bliss with the beloved object, at Margate,
Ramsgate, or Gravesend.

In 1842 Dickens wrote to Forster from Broadstairs :

Strange as it may appear to you the sea is
running so high that we have no choice but to
return by land.   No steamer can come out of
Ramsgate, and the Margate boat lay out all
night on Wednesday with all her passengers on
board.   You may be sure of us therefore on
Saturday at 5, for I have determined to leave
here to-morrow, as we could not otherwise
manage it in time ; and have engaged an

omnibus to bring the whole caravan by the
overland route. . . . We cannot open a
window, or a door ; legs are of no use on the
terrace ; and the Margate boats can only take
people aboard at Herne Bay !

And in 1849, on the 15th July, also from Broadstairs,
he wrote, " I propose to return to town by boat
from Ramsgate."

On one occasion when he had returned to Broadstairs from London via Margate, Forster tells us,
" it had been arranged that his wife should meet
him at Margate ; but he had walked impatiently
far beyond the place for meeting when at last he
caught sight of her, not in a small chaise but in a
large carriage and pair followed by an excited
crowd, and with the youth that should have been
driving the little pony bruised and bandaged on the
box behind the two prancing horses.   ' You may
faintly imagine my amazement at encountering
this carriage, and the strange people, and Kate,
and the crowd, and the bandaged one, and all the
rest of it.'   And than in a line or two I had the
story " :

> At the top of a steep hill on the road, with a
> ditch on each side, the pony bolted, whereupon
> what does John do but jump out ! He says he
> was thrown out, but it cannot be.   The reins
> immediately became entangled in the wheels,
> and away went the pony down the hill madly,
> with Kate inside rending the Isle of Thanet with
> her screams.   The accident might have been a
> fearful one, if the pony had not, Thank Heaven,
> on getting to the bottom, pitched over the side ;
> breaking the shaft and cutting her hind legs,
> but in the most extraordinary manner smashing
> her own way apart.   She tumbled down, a

bundle of legs with her head tucked underneath,
and left the chaise standing on the bank ! A
Captain Devaynes and his wife were passing in
their carriage at the moment, saw the accident
with no power of preventing it, got Kate out,
laid her on the grass, and behaved with infinite
kindness. All's well that ends well, and I
think she's really none the worse for the fright.
John is in bed a good deal bruised, but without
any broken bone, and likely soon to come right ;
though for the present plastered all over, and,
like Squeers, a brown-paper parcel chock-full of
nothing but groans. The women generally have
no sympathy for him whatever, and the nurse
says, with indignation, How could he go and
leave a unprotected female in the shay !

IV

Another well-known Thanet seaside town is
Herne Bay ; but we have no record that Dickens
ever visited it. In a letter to Douglas Jerrold,
written on a cold wet day in June, 1843, he dis-
misses the proposal of a visit there, rather curtly :

Herne Bay. Hum. I suppose it's no worse
than any other place in this weather, but it is
watery rather—isn't it ? In my mind's eye,
I have the sea in a perpetual state of smallpox ;
and the chalk running downhill like town milk.
But I know the comfort of getting to work in a
fresh place, and proposing pious projects to
one's self, and having the more substantial
advantage of going to bed early and getting
up ditto, and walking about alone. I should
like to deprive you of the last-named happiness,
and to take a good long stroll, terminating in a

public-house, and whatever they chanced to have in it. But fine days are over, I think. The horrible misery of London in this weather, with not even a fire to make it cheerful, is hideous.

CHAPTER XIII

DOVER, DEAL AND FOLKESTONE

" There are two ways of going to Folkestone, both lovely and striking."

(Letter to Miss Boyle)

I

LIKE little David Copperfield we have at length reached Dover, the destination heralded so often in the quotations given in the previous chapters ; the destination so often of Dickens himself on his way to the Continent, where he spent several months of the years between 1844 and 1856.

There is, however, no record of his having stayed for any length of time in Dover until 1852, three years after he had introduced it by name (with Broadstairs in his mind all the time) as the place where Betsey Trotwood lived.

When David Copperfield decided to run away from the terror of the bottle factory, he made enquiry of his old nurse Peggotty as to the place of residence of the aunt, of whom he had heard, who had taken so much umbrage at his being a boy as never to take any further notice of him or his mother.

Peggotty's answer soon arrived, and was, as usual, full of affectionate devotion. She enclosed the half guinea (I was afraid she must have had a world of trouble to get it out of Mr. Barkis's box), and told me that Miss Betsey lived near Dover, but whether at Dover itself, at Hythe, Sandgate, or Folkestone, she could not say. One of our men, however, informing me on my asking him about these places, that they were all close together, I deemed this enough for my object, and resolved to set out at the end of that week.

We have followed poor David through his sorrowful tramp along the Dover Road and are now in the town of his desire.

When I came, at last, upon the bare, wide downs near Dover, it relieved the solitary aspect of the scene with hope ; and not until I reached that first great aim of my journey, and actually set foot in the town itself, on the sixth day of my flight, did it desert me. But then, strange to say, when I stood with my ragged shoes, and my dusty, sunburnt, half-clothed figure, in the place so long desired, it seemed to vanish like a dream, and to leave me helpless and dispirited.

I inquired about my aunt among the boatmen first, and received various answers. One said she lived in the South Foreland Light, and had singed her whiskers by doing so ; another, that she was made fast to the great buoy outside the harbour, and could only be visited at half-tide ; a third, that she was locked up in Maidstone Jail for child-stealing ; a fourth, that she was seen to mount a broom, in the last high wind, and make direct for Calais. The fly-drivers, among whom I inquired next, were equally jocose and equally disrespectful ; and the shopkeepers, not liking my appearance, generally replied, without hearing what I had to say, that they had got nothing for me. I felt more miserable and destitute than

I had done at any period of my running away. My money was all gone, I had nothing left to dispose of ; I was hungry, thirsty, and worn out ; and seemed as distant from my end as if I had remained in London.

The morning had worn away in these inquiries, and I was sitting on the step of an empty shop at a street corner, near the market-place, deliberating upon wandering towards those other places which had been mentioned, when a fly-driver, coming by with his carriage, dropped a horsecloth. Something good-natured in the man's face, as I handed it up, encouraged me to ask him if he could tell me where Miss Trotwood lived ; though I had asked the question so often, that it almost died upon my lips.

" Trotwood," said he ; " let me see. I know the name, too. Old lady ? "

" Yes," I said, " rather."

" Pretty stiff in the back ? " said he, making himself upright.

" Yes," I said. " I should think it very likely."

" Carries a bag ? " said he : " bag with a good deal of room in it ; is gruffish, and comes down upon you, sharp ? "

My heart sank within me as I acknowledged the undoubted accuracy of this description.

" Why then, I tell you what," said he. " If you go up there," pointing with his whip towards the heights, " and keep right on till you come to some houses facing the sea, I think you'll hear of her. My opinion is, she won't stand anything, so here's a penny for you."

The " empty shop at a street corner, near the market-place " referred to above is claimed to be that of a firm of bakers, Messrs. Igglesden and Greaves ; and so great is the attachment that they have fixed a tablet to their new premises, on the site of the old shop, worded as follows :

Here
is the site of the steps
on which
Charles Dickens
represents
David Copperfield
as resting in his
search for his aunt
Betsey Trotwood

I accepted the gift thankfully, and bought a loaf with it. Dispatching this refreshment by the way, I went in the direction my friend had indicated, and walked on a good distance without coming to the houses he had mentioned. At length I saw some before me ; and approaching them, went into a little shop (it was what we used to call a general shop, at home), and inquired if they could have the goodness to tell me where Miss Trotwood lived. I addressed myself to a man behind the counter, who was weighing some rice for a young woman ; but the latter, taking the inquiry to herself, turned round quickly.

" My mistress ? " she said. " What do you want with her, boy ? "

" I want," I replied, " to speak to her, if you please."

" To beg of her, you mean," retorted the damsel.

" No," I said, " indeed." But suddenly remembering that in truth I came for no other purpose, I held my peace in confusion, and felt my face burn.

My aunt's handmaid, as I supposed she was from what she had said, put her rice in a little basket and walked out of the shop ; telling me that I could follow her, if I wanted to know where Miss Trotwood lived. I needed no second permission ; though I was by this time in such a state of consternation and agitation, that my legs shook under me. I followed the young woman, and we soon came to a very neat little cottage with cheerful bow-windows : in front of it, a small square gravelled court or garden full of flowers, carefully tended, and smelling deliciously.

" This is Miss Trotwood's," said the young woman. " Now you know ; and that's all I have got to say." With which words she hurried into the house, as if to shake off the responsibility of my appearance ; and left me standing at the garden-gate, looking disconsolately over the top of it towards the parlour-window, where a muslin curtain partly undrawn in the middle, a large round green screen or fan fastened on to the window-sill, a small table, and a great chair, suggested to me that my aunt might be at that moment seated in awful state.

My shoes were by this time in a woeful condition. The soles had shed themselves bit by bit, and the upper leathers had broken and burst until the very shape and form of shoes had departed from them. My hat (which had served me for a nightcap too) was so crushed and bent, that no old battered handleless saucepan on a dunghill need have been ashamed to vie with it.

My shirt and trousers, stained with heat, dew
grass, and the Kentish soil on which I had slept
—and torn besides—might have frightened the
birds from my aunt's garden, as I stood at the
gate. My hair had known no comb or brush
since I left London. My face, neck, and hands,
from unaccustomed exposure to the air and sun,
were burnt to a berry-brown. From head to
foot I was powdered almost as white with chalk
and dust, as if I had come out of a limekiln.
In this plight, and with a strong consciousness
of it, I waited to introduce myself to, and make
my first impression on, my formidable aunt.

There is no cottage at Dover that can be said to
have been the original of that of Miss Trotwood.
It is thought probable that Dickens simply transferred the locale from Broadstairs, as we have
stated on page 190.

The visit above referred to was for three months,
and he lived at 10, Camden Crescent, and wrote
part of *Bleak House* there. In this book appears a
reference to Dover Castle out of the mouth of
Mrs. Bagnet :

" Why, then, miss,' the old girl proceeded,
untying the strings of her bonnet for more air,
" you could as soon move Dover Castle as move
George on this point, unless you had got a new
power to move him with. And I have got it ! "

During this visit he wrote to Mary Boyle (22nd
July, 1852) :

My dear Mary, you do scant justice to Dover.
It is not quite a place to my taste, being too
bandy (I mean musical, no reference to its legs)
and infinitely too genteel. But the sea is very
fine, and the walks are quite remarkable. There
are two ways of going to Folkestone, both

lovely and striking in the highest degree ; and
there are heights and downs, and country roads,
and I don't know what, everywhere.

II

In April and May, 1856, he was again at Dover
for a short time, for we find him writing to Wilkie
Collins from the Ship Hotel and to Miss Hogarth
from the same place ; in his letter to the latter he
wrote :

I went to the Dover Theatre on Friday night,
which was a miserable spectacle. The pit is
boarded over, and it is a drinking and smoking
place. It was " for the benefit of Mrs. . . ."
and the town had been very extensively
placarded with " Don't forget Friday." I made
out four and ninepence (I am serious) in the
house, when I went in. We may have warmed
up in the course of the evening to twelve shillings.
A Jew played the grand piano ; Mrs. . . . sang
no end of songs (with not a bad voice, poor
creature) ; Mr. . . . sang comic songs fearfully,.
and danced clog hornpipes capitally ; and a
miserable woman, shivering in a shawl and
bonnet, sat in the side-boxes all the evening,
nursing Master . . . aged seven months. It
was a most forlorn business and I should have
contributed a sovereign to the treasury, if I had
known how.

I walked to Deal and back that day, and on
the previous day walked over the downs towards
Canterbury in a gale of wind. It was better
than still weather after all, being wonderfully
fresh and free.

At the same time he wrote to his wife :

I did nothing at Dover (except for *Household Words*) and have not begun *Little Dorrit* No. 8 yet. But I took twenty-mile walks in the fresh air, and perhaps in the long run did better than if I had been at work.

The Ship undoubtedly stood for the Royal George Hotel referred to at length in *A Tale of Two Cities* :

When the mail got successfully to Dover, in the course of the forenoon, the head drawer at the Royal George Hotel opened the coach-door as his custom was. He did it with some flourish of ceremony, for a mail journey from London in ·winter was an achievement to congratulate an adventurous traveller upon.

By that time, there was only one adventurous traveller left to be congratulated : for the two others had been set down at their respective roadside destinations. The mildewy inside of the coach, with its damp and dirty straw, its disagreeable smell, and its obscurity, was rather like a larger dog-kennel. Mr. Lorry, the passenger, shaking himself out of it in chains of straw, a tangle of shaggy wrapper, flapping hat, and muddy legs, was rather like a larger sort of dog.

" There will be a packet to Calais, to-morrow, drawer ? "

" Yes, sir, if the weather holds and the wind sets tolerable fair. The tide will serve pretty nicely at about two in the afternoon, sir. Bed, sir ? "

" I shall not go to bed till night ; but I want a bedroom and a barber."

" And then breakfast, sir ? Yes, sir. That way, sir, if you please. Show Concord ! Gentle-

man's valise and hot water to Concord.   Pull off
gentleman's boots in Concord.   (You will find
a fine sea-coal fire, sir.)   Fetch barber to
Concord.   Stir about there, now, for Concord ! "

The Concord bed-chamber being always
assigned to a passenger by the mail, and
passengers by the mail being always heavily
wrapped up from head to foot, the room had
the odd interest for the establishment of the
Royal George, that although but one kind of
man was seen to go into it, all kinds and varieties
of men came out of it.   Consequently, another
drawer, and two porters, and several maids and
the landlady, were all loitering by accident at
various points of the road between the Concord
and the coffee-room, when a gentleman of sixty,
formally dressed in a brown suit of clothes,
pretty well worn, but very well kept, with large
square cuffs and large flaps to the pockets,
passed along on his way to his breakfast.

An account of the town of Dover appears in
Chapter IV of *A Tale of Two Cities*, written in 1859 :

When Mr. Lorry had finished his breakfast,
he went out for a stroll on the beach.   The little
narrow, crooked town of Dover hid itself away
from the beach, and ran its head into the chalk
cliffs, like a marine ostrich.   The beach was a
desert of heaps of sea and stones tumbling wildly
about, and the sea did what it liked, and what
it liked was destruction.   It thundered at the
town, and thundered at the cliffs, and brought
the coast down, madly.   The air among the
houses was of so strong a piscatory flavour that
one might have supposed sick fish went up to be
dipped in it, as sick people went down to be
dipped in the sea.   A little fishing was done in

the port, and a quantity of strolling about by night, and looking seaward : particularly at those times when the tide made, and was near flood. Small tradesmen, who did no business whatever, sometimes unaccountably realised large fortunes, and it was remarkable that nobody in the neighbourhood could endure a lamplighter.

After Dickens visited the Ship in 1856, it was rebuilt and renamed the Lord Warden, from which on the 24th May, 1861, we find Dickens writing to Wilkie Collins :

Of course I am dull and penitent here, but it is very beautiful. I can work well, and I walked, by the cliffs, to Folkestone and back to-day, when it was so exquisitely beautiful that, though I was alone, I could not keep silence on the subject. In the fourteen miles I doubt if I met twelve people.

In the following November he gave a reading at Dover and described the audience as that with the greatest sense of humour, in a letter to Miss Hogarth :

The effect of the readings at Hastings and Dover really seems to have outdone the best usual impression ; and at Dover they wouldn't go, but sat applauding like mad. . . . The audience with the greatest sense of humour, certainly is Dover. The people in the stalls set the example of laughing, in the most curiously unreserved way ; and they laughed with such really cordial enjoyment, when Squeers read the boys' letters, that the contagion extended to me. For, one couldn't hear them without laughing too. . . . So, I am thankful to say, all goes well, and the recompense for the trouble is in every way Great.

The same letter gave an interesting account of a heavy sea experienced here during a great storm that was at that time sweeping round the coast :

The bad weather has not in the least touched us, and the storm was most magnificent at Dover. All the great side of the Lord Warden next to the sea had to be emptied, the break of the waves was so prodigious, and the noise so utterly confounding. The sea came in like a great sky of immense clouds, for ever breaking suddenly into furious rain ; all kinds of wreck were washed in, among other things a very pretty brass-bound chest being thrown about like a feather. . . . The unhappy Ostend packet, unable to get in or go back, beat about the Channel all Tuesday night and until noon yesterday, when I saw her come in, with five men at the wheel, a picture of misery inconceivable.

In " The Calais Night Mail " (*The Uncommercial Traveller*) he tells us :

When I first made the acquaintance of Calais it was as a maundering young wretch . . . conscious of no extremities but the one great extremity—sea sickness— . . . who had been put into a horrible swing at Dover Harbour and had tumbled giddily out of it on the French Coast.

This was a confession made in 1863, on which occasion he goes on to speak more generally of Dover :

I have my animosities towards Dover. I particularly detest Dover for the self-complacency with which it goes to bed. It always goes to bed (when I am going to Calais) with a more brilliant display of lamp and candle than any other town. Mr. and Mrs. Birmingham, host and hostess of the Lord Warden Hotel, are my much esteemed friends, but they are too conceited about the comforts of that establishment when the Night Mail is starting. I know it is a good house to stay at, and I don't want the fact insisted upon in all its warm bright windows at such an hour. I know the Warden is a stationary edifice that never rolls or pitches, and I object to its big outline seeming to insist upon that circumstance, and, as it were, to come over me with it, when I am reeling on the deck of the boat. Beshrew the Warden likewise, for obstructing that corner, and making the wind so angry as it rushes round. Shall I not know that it blows quite soon enough, without the officious Warden's interference ?

As I wait here on board the night packet, for the South Eastern Train to come down with the Mail, Dover appears to me to be illuminated for some intensely aggravating festivity in my personal dishonour. All its noises smack of taunting praises of the land, and dispraises of the gloomy sea, and of me for going on it. The drums upon the heights have gone to bed, or I know they would rattle taunts against me for having my unsteady footing on this slippery deck. The many gas eyes of the Marine Parade twinkle in an offensive manner, as if with derision. The distant dogs of Dover bark at me in my mis-shapen wrappers, as if I were Richard the Third.

A screech, a bell, and two red eyes come gliding down the Admiralty Pier with a smoothness of motion rendered more smooth by the heaving of the boat. The sea makes noises against the pier, as if several hippopotami were

lapping at it, and were prevented by circumstances over which they had no control from
drinking peaceably. We, the boat, become
violently agitated—rumble, hum, scream, roar,
and establish an immense family washing-day
at each paddle-box. Bright patches break out
in the train as the doors of the post-office vans
are opened, and instantly stooping figures with
sacks upon their backs begin to be beheld among
the piles, descending as it would seem in ghostly
procession to Davy Jones's Locker. The
passengers come on board ; a few shadowy
Frenchmen, with hatboxes shaped like the
stoppers of gigantic case-bottles ; a few shadowy
Germans in immense fur coats and boots ; a
few shadowy Englishmen prepared for the worst
and pretending not to expect it. I cannot
disguise from my uncommercial mind the
miserable fact that we are a body of outcasts ;
that the attendants on us are as scant in number
as may serve to get rid of us with the least
possible delay ; that there are no night-loungers
interested in us ; that the unwilling lamps
shiver and shudder at us ; that the sole object
is to commit us to the deep and abandon us.
Lo, the two red eyes glaring in increasing
distance, and then the very train itself has gone
to bed before we are off !

III

The neighbouring town of Deal is introduced into
Bleak House, where Esther Summerson says :
    I could only suggest that I should go down to
Deal where Richard was then stationed. . . .
We all went to London that afternoon and

finding two places on the mail, secured them. At our usual bed-time Charley and I were rolling away seaward, with the Kentish letters. . . .

At last we came into the narrow streets of Deal and very gloomy they were, upon a raw misty morning. The long flat beach with its little irregular houses, wooden and brick, and its litter of capstans, and great boats and sheds, and bare upright poles with tackle and blocks, and loose gravelly waste places overgrown with grass and weeds, were as dull an appearance as any place I ever saw. The sea was heaving under a thick white fog ; and nothing else was moving but a few early ropemakers, who with the yarn twisted round their bodies, looked as if, tired of their present state of existence, they were spinning themselves into cordage.

But when we got into a warm room in an excellent hotel . . . Deal began to look more cheerful. Our little room was like a ship's cabin, and that delighted Charley very much.

It was while walking on the beach at Deal that Esther witnessed a small boat landing from a " great Indiaman " and recognized among the officers Allan Woodcourt, returned from the East, with whom she later had an interview at the hotel.

Deal was probably the town mentioned in " Out of the Season," to which he walked from " the watering-place out of the season " :

A walk of ten miles brought me to a seaside town without a cliff, which, like the town I had come from, was out of the season too. Half of the houses were shut up ; half of the other half were to let ; the town might have done as much business as it was doing then, if it had been at the bottom of the sea. Nobody seemed to flourish save the attorney ; his clerk's pen was going in the bow-window of his wooden house ; his brass door-plate alone was free from salt, and had been polished up that morning. On the beach, among the rough luggers and capstans, groups of storm-beaten boatmen, like a sort of marine monsters, watched under the lee of those objects, or stood leaning forward against the wind, looking out through battered spy-glasses. The parlour bell in the Admiral Benbow had grown so flat with being out of the season, that neither could I hear it ring when I pulled the handle for lunch, nor could the young woman in black stockings and strong shoes, who acted as waiter out of the season, until it had been tinkled three times.

Admiral Benbow's cheese was out of the season, but his home-made bread was good, and his beer was perfect. Deluded by some earlier spring day which had been warm and sunny, the Admiral had cleared the firing out of his parlour stove, and had put some flower-pots in—which was amiable and hopeful in the Admiral, but not judicious : the room being, at that present visiting, transcendantly cold. I therefore took the liberty of peeping out across a little stone passage into the Admiral's kitchen, and, seeing a high settle with its back towards me drawn out in front of the Admiral's kitchen fire, I strolled in, bread and cheese in hand, munching and looking about. One landsman and two boatmen were seated on the settle, smoking pipes and drinking beer out of thick pint crockery mugs—mugs peculiar to such places, with parti-coloured rings round them, and ornaments between the rings like frayed-out roots.

IV

Although it was not until 1855 that Dickens spent a seaside holiday at Folkestone, the place was well known to him before, and had often been visited during his holidays at Broadstairs.

On 13th July, 1849, we find him writing from Broadstairs :

"Why sir, I'm going to Folkestone on Saturday, sir, not on accounts of the manifacktring of Bengal cheroots as there is there, but for the survay in ' o ' the coast sir. 'Cos you see sir, bein' here sir, and not a finishing my work sir till to-morrow sir, I couldn't go afore ! And if I was to come home and not go, and come back agin sir, wy, it would be nat'urally a hulluxing of myself sir. Yes, sir. . . . If you was to come down . . . sir, by the train as gits to Folkestone twenty minutes ater five, you'd find me smoking a Bengal cheroot on the platform. You couldn't spend your arternoon better sir. Dover, Sandgate, Herne Bay—they're all to be wisited sir."

"There are two ways of going to Folkestone," he wrote to Mary Boyle from Dover in 1852, " both lovely and striking in the highest degree, and there are heights and downs and country roads, and I don't know what, everywhere."

In the summer of 1855 Dickens and his family took residence at No. 3 Albion Villas, Folkestone, and it was during his stay there that he decided to give a public reading from his works to assist the funds of the local institutes ; this led to the idea of giving such readings for his own benefit, the first series of which was given three years later.

Thus we find him writing to Forster from Folkestone on the 16th September, 1855 : " I am going

15

to read for them here, on the 5th of next month, and
have answered in the last fortnight thirty applica-
tions to do the like all over England, Ireland and
Scotland." And a week later :

I am going to read here next Friday week.
There are (as there are everywhere) a Literary
Institution and a Working Men's Institution,
which have not the slightest sympathy or connection. The stalls are five shillings, and I
have made them fix the working men's admission
at three pence, and I hope it may bring them
together. The event comes off in a carpenter's
shop, as the biggest place that can be got.

We cannot glean very much of Dickens's life at
Folkestone from the published letters, as very few
have reference to it, but an interesting account of
the launching of a boat is given in a letter to Wilkie
Collins dated 30th September, 1855 :

They launched the boat, the rapid building
of which you remember, the other day. All the
fishermen in the place, all the nondescripts, and
all the boys pulled at it with ropes from six a.m.
to four p.m. Every now and then the ropes
broke, and they all fell down in the shingle.
The obstinate way in which the beastly thing
wouldn't move was so exasperating that I
wondered they didn't shoot it, or burn it.
Whenever it moved an inch they all cheered ;
whenever it wouldn't move they all swore.
Finally, when it was quite given over, some one
tumbled against it accidentally (as it appeared
to me, looking out at my window here) and it
instantly shot about a mile into the sea, and they
all stood looking at it helplessly.

To Macready he wrote on the 4th October, 1855, of
having a horrible temptation when I lay down

my book-pen, to run out on the breezy downs here, tear up the hills, slide down the same, and conduct myself in a frenzied manner for the relief that only exercise gives me.

The only reference of importance to Folkestone in the works are to be found in *Reprinted Pieces*. The paper originally appeared in *Household Words* 30th August, 1851. The following extract is from " A Flight," describing the journey by train from London to Folkestone to connect with the steamer for Boulogne :

Now fresher air, now glimpses of unenclosed Downland with flapping crows flying over it . . . now the sea, now Folkestone. . . . We are dropped slowly down to the Port, and sidle to and fro (the whole Train) before the insensible Royal George Hotel for some ten minutes. The Royal George takes no more heed of us than its namesake under water at Spithead, or under earth at Windsor, does. The Royal George dog lies winking and blinking at us, without taking the trouble to sit up ; and the Royal George's " wedding party " at the open window (who seem, I must say, rather tired of bliss) don't bestow a solitary glance upon us. . . . The first gentleman in Folkestone is evidently used up, on this subject.

There is no Royal George Hotel at Folkestone. Some years later, in writing *A Tale of Two Cities* Dickens calls the Ship Hotel at Dover, the Royal George (see page 217).

To *Household Words* of 29th September, 1855, Dickens contributed an article on Folkestone under the title of " Out of Town." In it he called the place Pavilionstone. This was subsequently published in *Reprinted Pieces* :

Sitting, on a bright September morning, among my books and papers at my open window on the cliff overhanging the sea-beach, I have the sky and ocean framed before me like a beautiful picture. A beautiful picture, but with such movement in it, such changes of light upon the sails of ships and wake of steamboats, such dazzling gleams of silver far out at sea, such fresh touches on the crisp wave-tops as they break and roll towards me—a picture with such music in the billowy rush upon the shingle, the blowing of morning wind through the corn-sheaves where the farmers' waggons are busy, the singing of the larks, and the distant voices of children at play—such charms of sight and sound as all the Galleries on earth can but poorly suggest.

So dreamy is the murmur of the sea below my window that I may have been here, for anything I know, one hundred years. Not that I have grown old, for, daily on the neighbouring downs and grassy hill-sides, I find that I can still in reason walk any distance, jump over anything, and climb up anywhere. . . .

The name of the little town, on whose shore this sea is murmuring . . . is Pavilionstone. Within a quarter of a century, it was a little fishing town, and they do say, that the time was, when it was a little smuggling town. I have heard that it was rather famous in the hollands and brandy way, and that coevally with that reputation the lamplighter's was considered a bad life at the Assurance offices. It was observed that if he were not particular about lighting up, he lived in peace ; but that, if he made the best of the oil-lamps in the steep and

narrow streets, he usually fell over the cliff at
an early age. Now, gas and electricity run to
the very water's edge, and the South Eastern
Railway Company screech at us in the dead of
night.

But, the old little fishing and smuggling town
remains, and is so tempting a place for the latter
purpose, that I think of going out some night
next week, in a fur cap and a pair of petticoat
trousers, and running an empty tub, as a kind of
archæological pursuit. Let nobody with corns
come to Pavilionstone, for there are breakneck
flights of ragged steps, connecting the principal
streets by back-ways, which will cripple that
visitor in half an hour. . . . In connection
with these breakneck steps I observe some
wooden cottages, with tumble-down out-houses,
and back-yards three feet square, adorned with
garlands of dried fish. . . . The South Eastern
Company have brought Pavilionstone into such
vogue with their tidal trains and splendid steam
packets, that a new Pavilionstone is rising up.
I am, myself, of New Pavilionstone. We are a
little mortary and limey at present, but we are
getting on capitally. . . . We are sensibly
laid out in general ; and with a little care and
pains (by no means wanting, so far), shall
become a very pretty place. We ought to be,
for our situation is delightful, our air is delicious,
and our breezy hills and downs, carpeted with
wild thyme, and decorated with millions of
wild flowers, are, on the faith of a pedestrian,
perfect. In New Pavilionstone we are a little
too much addicted to small windows with more
bricks in them than glass, . . . and we get
unexpected sea-views through cracks in the

street doors ; on the whole, however, we are
very snug and comfortable, and well accom-
modated. . . .

The lion of Pavilionstone is its Great Hotel.
A dozen years ago, going over to Paris by South
Eastern Tidal Steamer you used to be dropped
upon the platform of the main line Pavilionstone Station (not a junction then) at eleven
o'clock on a dark winter's night, in a roaring
wind ; and in the howling wilderness outside the
station, was a short omnibus which brought you
up by the forehead the instant you got in at the
door ; and nobody cared about you, and you
were alone in the world. You bumped over
infinite chalk, until you were turned out at a
strange building which had just left off being a
barn without having quite begun to be a house,
where nobody expected your coming, or knew
what to do with you when you were come, and
where you were usually blown about, until you
happened to be blown against the cold beef, and
finally into bed. . . .

Now you come down to Pavilionstone in a
free and easy manner. . . . If you are going
to our Great Pavilionstone Hotel, the spright-
liest porters under the sun, whose cheerful looks
are a pleasant welcome, shoulder your luggage,
drive it off in vans, bowl it away in trucks, and
enjoy themselves in playing athletic games with
it. If you are for public life at our great
Pavilionstone Hotel, you walk into that establishment as if it were your club ; and find ready
for you, your news-room, dining-room, smoking-
room, billiard-room, music-room, public breakfast, public dinner twice a-day (one plain, one
gorgeous), hot baths and cold baths. . . .

A thoroughly good inn, in the days of coaching and posting, was a noble place. But no such inn would have been equal to the reception of four or five hundred people, all of them wet through, and half of them dead sick, every day in the year. This is where we shine, in our Pavilionstone Hotel. Again—who, coming and going, pitching and tossing, boating and training, hurrying in, and flying out could ever have calculated the fees to be paid at an old-fashioned house ?   In our Pavilionstone Hotel vocabulary, there is no such word as fee. Everything is done for you ; every service is provided at a fixed and reasonable charge ; all the prices are hung up in all the rooms ; and you can make out your own bill beforehand, as well as the book-keeper. . . .

The following year Dickens wrote another seaside article, " Out of the Season," already referred to. Folkestone was probably the " watering-place out of the season " that he had in his mind, although no mention is made of it by name. He tells us how he vainly tried to write a chapter, but the heavy wind reminded him he ought to have a blow :

So I gave up the magnificent chapter for that day, entirely persuading myself that I was under a moral obligation to have a blow.

I had a good one, and that on the high road —the very high road, on the top of the cliffs, where I met the stage-coach with all the out-sides holding their hats on and themselves too, and overtook a flock of sheep with the wool about their necks blown into such great ruffs that they looked like fleecy owls. The wind played upon the lighthouse as if it were a great whistle, the

spray was driven over the sea in a cloud of haze,
the ships rolled and pitched heavily, and at
intervals long slants and flaws of light made
mountain-steeps of communication between the
ocean and the sky.

At length, the full conviction was on him " that
the day for the great chapter was at last arrived " :
It had fallen calm, however, in the night, and
as I sat at breakfast I blushed to remember that
I had not yet been on the Downs ! Really, on
so quiet and bright a morning this must be set
right. As an essential part of the Whole Duty
of Man, therefore, I left the chapter to itself—
for the present—and went on the Downs. They
were wonderfully green and beautiful, and gave
me a good deal to do. When I had done with
the free air and the view, I had to go down into
the valley and look after the hops (which I
know nothing about), and to be equally solicitous
as to the cherry orchards. Then I took it on
myself to cross-examine a tramping family in
black (mother alleged, I have no doubt by
herself in person, to have died last week), and
to accompany eighteen-pence which produced a
great effect, with moral admonitions which
produced none at all. Finally, it was late in the
afternoon before I got back to the unprecedented
chapter, and then I determined that it was out
of the season, as the place was, and put it away.

CHAPTER XIV

TUNBRIDGE WELLS, ASHFORD AND MINSTER

" Among the Kentish Hops and Harvest."
("A Flight" : *Reprinted Pieces*)

To Tunbridge Wells there are only one or two passing references in the works of Dickens, although he undoubtedly had more than a passing acquaintance with it. It is somewhat strange that this beautiful and historic health resort was not introduced more prominently into one or other of his stories.

Tavistock House,
Sixth June, 1854.

MY DEAR COLLINS,

Day	Thursday
Hour	Quarter past 11 a.m.
Place	Dover Terminus, London Bridge
Destination	Tunbridge Wells
Description of Railway Qualification	Return Ticket
(Signed)	Charles Dickens
Ent'd.	

(side text) Form of trip appointment, in compliance with Act of Parliament, Victoria, cap 7, sec. 304.

233

The characteristic letter on the preceding page, written to Wilkie Collins, shows us that these two friends made Tunbridge Wells a venue on at least one occasion.

In *Reprinted Pieces*, in the paper entitled "A Flight," reprinted from *Household Words* of 30th August, 1851, there is an account of a train journey through Kent, passing Tunbridge Wells and Ashford :

> I fly away among the Kentish hops and harvest. What do *I* care ? Bang ! We have let another Station off, and fly away regardless. Everything is flying. The hop-gardens turn gracefully towards me, presenting regular avenues of hops in rapid flight, then whirl away. So do the pools and rushes, haystacks, sheep, clover in full bloom delicious to the sight and smell, corn-sheaves, cherry-orchards, apple-orchards, reapers, gleaners, hedges, gates, fields, that taper off into little angular corners, cottages, gardens, now and then a church. Bang, bang ! A double-barrelled Station ! Now a wood, now a bridge, now a landscape, now a cutting, now a—Bang ! a single-barrelled Station—there was a cricket-match somewhere with two white tents, and then four flying cows, then turnips—now the wires of the electric telegraph are all alive, and spin, and blurr their edges, and go up and down, and make the intervals between each other most irregular : contracting and expanding in the strangest manner. Now we slacken. With a screwing, and a grinding, and a smell of water thrown on ashes, now we stop !

> .   .   .   .   .

> Collected Guard appears. "Are you for Tunbridge, sir ? "

" Tunbridge ? No. Paris."

" Plenty of time, sir. No hurry. Five minutes here, sir, for refreshment."

. . . .

Flight resumed. Corn-sheaves, hop-gardens, reapers, gleaners, apple-orchards, cherry-orchards, Stations single and double-barrelled, Ashford.

Miss Twinkleton in *Edwin Drood* had very tender recollections of " The Wells " :

A certain season at Tunbridge Wells (airily called by Miss Twinkleton in this state of her existence " The Wells ") notably the season wherein a certain finished gentleman (compassionately called by Miss Twinkleton, in this stage of her existence, " Foolish Mr. Porters ") revealed a homage of the heart, whereof Miss Twinkleton, in her scholastic state of existence, is as ignorant as a granite pillar.

Another Kentish town visited by Dickens and Wilkie Collins was Ashford, mentioned above. In a letter dated 24th March, 1855, we find Dickens writing :

The train (an express one) leaves London Bridge Station on Tuesday at half past 11 in the forenoon. Fire and comfort are ordered to be in readiness at the inn at Ashford. We shall have to return at half past 2 in the morning, getting to town before 5.

Mr. Chestle, the fortunate choice of the elder Miss Larkins, described himself to David Copperfield as a grower of hops, with a " place " in the neighbourhood of Ashford, so Dickens's interest in the centre of the hop-growing district found a permanent record in his best-beloved book.

The little town of Minster in Sheppey, which overlooks the Marshes at the confluence of the Medway with the Thames, claims an association with Dickens. The Abbey Church there has been suggested as having been in Dickens's mind when he was referring to the last resting-place of Little Nell. True it is that the location of the church does not fit in with the story, and there is not very much evidence to show that Dickens had ever visited Tong in Shropshire, which is generally supposed to be the village which was the end of the long journey of Little Nell and her grandfather ; but Forster states that as a boy Dickens more than once accompanied his father in the pay yacht to Sheerness, which is quite adjacent. Mr. Henry Harbour in his guide to Sheerness writes : " The great story teller was often at Minster visiting a friend at Prospect Villa which stands opposite the banker's at the foot of the hill."

The Antiquary for March, 1910, makes the suggestion that in putting these words into the mouth of the kind schoolmaster in *The Old Curiosity Shop*—

Do you think there are no deeds far away from here, in which these dead may be best remembered ? Nell, Nell, there may be people busy in this world at this instant, in whose good actions and good thoughts these very graves, neglected as they look to us, are the chief instruments—

Dickens was thinking of Minster Abbey, where there is a brass before the altar, to the sole sponsor to the Kentish Charter of 1293, a forerunner of Wat Tyler in 1381.

And so our exploration of the Kent of Dickens is over. No other county of England has such a store of memories with one man of letters ; no other county was held in such esteem by Dickens. The writer hopes to cover the remainder of the England of Dickens in a subsequent volume.

KENT IN THE NOVELS OF DICKENS

Sketches by Boz (1833–36)
    Steam Excursion (1834)
        Gravesend
        Margate
    Watkins Tottle (1835)
        Ramsgate
    Our Parish (1835)
        Chatham
    The Tuggses at Ramsgate
    (1836)
        Gravesend
        Ramsgate
        Margate
        Pegwell Bay
    The Great Winglebury Duel
    (1836)
        Rochester
            High Street
            Town Hall
            Winglebury Arms (Bull
             Hotel)
    Mudfog Papers (1837–38)
        Rochester
        Canterbury

The Pickwick Papers (1836–37)
    Chatham
    Cobham
    Dover Road
    Gravesend
    Maidstone
    Rochester
    Shorne

Oliver Twist (1837–38)
    Rochester (Mudfog)

Nicholas Nickleby (1838–39)
    Rochester (in preface)

Dombey and Son (1846–47)
    Kent
    Gravesend
    Chatham
    Dover Road

David Copperfield (1849–50)
    Blackheath
    Canterbury
    Chatham
    Dover
    Folkestone
    Gravesend
    Hythe
    Maidstone
    Medway River
    Rochester
    Sandgate
    South Foreland

Bleak House (1852–53)
    Deal
    Gravesend
    Kent

Hard Times (1854)
    Chatham

Little Dorrit (1855–56)
    Canterbury
    Dartford
    Dover Road
    Sittingbourne

A Tale of Two Cities (1859)
Chatham
Dover
Shooter's Hill

Great Expectations (1860–61)
Cooling Marshes
Rochester
Gravesend
Greenhithe

Our Mutual Friend (1864–65)
Blackheath
Chatham
Northfleet

Edwin Drood (1869–70)
Rochester (Cloisterham)

Christmas Books
A Christmas Carol (1843)
Gad's Hill
Rochester

Christmas Stories
Perils of Certain English Prisoners (1857)
Seven Poor Travellers (1854)
Chatham
Cobham
Maidstone
Rochester
Sheerness
Blackheath

Reprinted Pieces
A Child's Dream of a Star (1850)
Chatham

The Begging Letter Writer (1850)
Chatham
Our English Watering Place (1851)
Broadstairs
Out of Town (1855)
Folkestone
Out of the Season (1856)
Folkestone
Deal
The Detective Police (1850)
Chatham
A Flight (1851)
Ashford
Dover
Tunbridge Wells

The Uncommercial Traveller
Travelling Abroad (1860)
Blackheath
Canterbury
Chatham
Dover
Gravesend
Gad's Hill
Rochester
Shooter's Hill
Tramps (1860)
Cobham
Strood
Dover Road
Dullborough Town (1860)
Chatham
Rochester
Calais Night Mail (1863)
Dover
Chatham Dockyard (1863)
Chatham

INDEX TO PLACES